UNDERSTANDING BORDERLINE PERSONALITY DISORDER

THE STARTLING TRUTHS UNVEILED, A ROADMAP TO HEALING

MICHAEL GRANTWOOD

UNDERSTANDING BORDERLINE PERSONALITY DISORDER

MICHAEL DOWNWOOD

To the resilient souls who have sought truth amidst the shadows of stigma and misconceptions, who have refused to let a diagnosis define their worth, and who have shown the world the strength that lies within, this is for you.

Limited Liability - Disclaimer

Please note that the content of this book is based on personal experience and various information sources, and it is only for personal use.

Please note the information contained within this document is for educational and entertainment purposes only and no warranties of any kind are declared or implied.

Readers acknowledge that the author is not engaging in the rendering of legal, financial, or professional advice. Please consult a licensed professional before attempting any techniques outlined in this book.

CONTENTS

PREFACE

In the realm of understanding Borderline Personality Disorder (BPD), we find ourselves on a profound journey—a journey of unraveling complexities, dispelling misconceptions, and embracing empathy. As I stand on the precipice of this exploration, it is my honor to introduce you to a transformative book, "Understanding Borderline Personality Disorder: The Startling Truths Unveiled, A Roadmap to Healing," written by the esteemed author Michael Grantwood.

From the moment I delved into the pages of this manuscript, I knew that I had stumbled upon something extraordinary—a work of art crafted with compassion, insight, and a relentless pursuit of truth. It is with great pleasure that I write this preface, humbled by Michael Grantwood's unwavering dedication to shedding light on the intricacies of BPD and uplifting those affected by this disorder.

Within these pages, you will find a mosaic of personal narratives, scientific knowledge, and therapeutic insights, meticulously woven together to form a tapestry of understanding. Michael's ability to seamlessly blend personal experience with professional expertise is a testament to his commitment to authenticity and connection.

This book not only seeks to educate and inform but also to foster empathy and connection—a noble aspiration in a world where stigma and judgment often cast a shadow on those living with mental health challenges. By challenging prevailing narratives and debunking misconceptions, Michael invites us to step outside the confines of our preconceived notions and embrace the humanity that unites us all.

As I journeyed through the chapters of this book, I was struck by Michael's unwavering belief in the resilience and potential for growth within individuals living with BPD. He deftly guides readers towards a path of healing, offering practical tools, strategies, and exercises that empower and inspire.

But perhaps what struck me most was Michael's

capacity for compassion—their ability to hold space for the vulnerability and pain that often accompany BPD. It is through this lens of empathy that he encourages readers to embark on their own personal journeys of self-discovery, embracing the truth that healing is a unique and individual process.

To read this book is to embark on a pilgrimage—a pilgrimage towards understanding, acceptance, and profound transformation. It is an invitation to transcend the limitations of stigma and judgment and to foster a world where compassion and empathy prevail.

May this book find its way into the hands of those seeking solace, understanding, and hope. May it inspire mental health professionals to approach their work with renewed empathy and a commitment to ongoing growth. And may it challenge society at large to embrace a more compassionate and inclusive understanding of mental health.

In closing, I express my deepest gratitude to Michael Grantwood for his dedication, vulnerability, and unwavering commitment to the journey of healing. Through his words, he has touched countless lives and provided a guiding light for those navigating the complexities of BPD.

Now, dear reader, I invite you to step into the

world within these pages—a world where under-standing and healing await. Embrace the wisdom, insights, and transformative power that lie before you, and may your journey be filled with self-discovery, resilience, and profound growth.

Dr. Elizabeth Kingston

INTRODUCTION: THE JOURNEY BEGINS

Welcome to the captivating world of "Understanding Borderline Personality Disorder: The Startling Truths Unveiled, A Roadmap to Healing." As an esteemed expert in the field, I extend my hand to guide you through an illuminating journey of comprehension and profound transformation.

In the pages that follow, we will embark on a quest to unravel the intricate nature of Borderline Personality Disorder (BPD) and shatter the misconceptions and stigma that surround it. By delving into the depths of this disorder, we aim to empower you with a comprehensive understanding and equip you with the invaluable tools needed to navigate the challenges that BPD presents.

Understanding BPD is not only essential for individuals directly affected by the disorder but also for their loved ones, caregivers, and the broader mental health community. Through this exploration, we aspire to foster empathy, compassion, and acceptance for those touched by BPD.

Our journey of revelation begins by illuminating the fundamental truths that lie at the core of BPD. We will uncover the distinctive features and diagnostic criteria that define this disorder, providing clarity and context to its complexities. By unraveling the multifaceted nature of BPD, we hope to instill a sense of validation and validation for individuals grappling with its challenges.

As we venture deeper into this compelling odyssey, we will shed light on the startling truths that accompany BPD. We will explore the turbulent landscape of emotional dysregulation, where intense and rapidly shifting emotions can be overwhelming, leaving individuals feeling lost and disconnected from their own internal compass. Together, we will dissect the intricate dance of unstable self-image, examining how it shapes personal identity and influences one's perception of the world.

No exploration of BPD would be complete

without addressing the pervasive fear of abandonment that so often permeates the lives of those affected. We will delve into the profound impact this fear can have on relationships, self-worth, and overall well-being, unveiling strategies for healing and cultivating healthier connections.

At the heart of our journey lies the pervasive sense of emptiness that characterizes BPD. Together, we will navigate the depths of this emotional void, seeking understanding and pathways to fill it with purpose, self-discovery, and personal growth.

Throughout our exploration, we will traverse the minefield of common triggers that can ignite emotional turmoil and trigger the rollercoaster of mood swings. By understanding these triggers, we empower ourselves with knowledge and awareness, laying the groundwork for more stable emotional landscapes.

With each chapter that unfolds, we will piece together a comprehensive roadmap to healing—a tapestry of evidence-based approaches, practical strategies, and compassionate insights. This roadmap will guide you toward a place of self-acceptance, resilience, and transformation.

Together, we will embark on an extraordinary

journey. Let the pages of this book become a beacon of light, illuminating the path toward understanding, self-empowerment, and a life filled with hope and possibility. The road may be challenging, but I assure you that the rewards of this transformative journey are immeasurable.

1 UNVEILING THE STARTLING TRUTHS

"All great truths begin as blasphemies."

GEORGE BERNARD SHAW

---

n this compelling chapter, we embark on a profound exploration into the multifaceted realm of Borderline Personality Disorder (BPD). Our aim is to unravel the enigmatic truths that lie beneath the surface of this intricate condition. By immersing ourselves in a comprehensive understanding of BPD's core symptoms, deciphering the common triggers that ignite tumultuous emotional rollercoasters, and delving into the depths of self-harm and suicidal tendencies, we will shed light on this often-misunderstood disorder.

Borderline Personality Disorder is a complex mental health condition that manifests in various symptoms, significantly impacting an individual's emotional and behavioral functioning. At its core, BPD is a disorder characterized by intense emotional dysregulation, impulsive behaviors, turbulent relationships, and a distorted self-image. By unraveling these key features, we gain valuable insights into the challenges faced by individuals grappling with BPD, ultimately fostering empathy and understanding.

Emotional dysregulation lies at the heart of BPD, giving rise to a torrential storm of ever-shifting emotions. Individuals with BPD experience a tumultuous internal landscape, oscillating between profound joy and euphoria to the depths of despair, anger, or a pervasive sense of emptiness. These emotional fluctuations, often swift and intense, generate significant distress and can strain the capacity to sustain stable relationships.

Impulsivity, another hallmark trait of BPD, compels individuals to engage in impulsive and potentially self-destructive behaviors. From substance abuse to binge eating, reckless driving to compulsive shopping, these impulsive actions serve as temporary salves, momentarily alleviating emotional pain or providing a fleeting sense of control. However, they invariably exacerbate the underlying challenges faced by individuals with BPD.

Stability in relationships proves elusive for those with BPD. The fear of abandonment, an omnipresent specter, permeates their interactions with others. Trust becomes a fragile concept, and the constant dread of rejection engenders a tumultuous love-hate dynamic within relationships. Intense periods of idealization, followed by abrupt devaluation, lead to a rollercoaster of emotions, exacerbating the complexities of maintaining stable connections.

A distorted self-image, a profound sense of uncertainty regarding one's identity, values, and aspirations, plagues individuals with BPD. The struggle to define oneself, the malleability of goals and aspirations, and the constant quest for a stable sense of identity contribute to the complexity of this disorder. It is within this labyrinth of self-identity that individuals with BPD navigate, often accompanied by feelings of confusion and instability.

As we delve deeper into the truths that surround BPD, we will confront the common triggers that set off emotional rollercoasters. Themes such as abandonment, rejection, criticism, and the intensity of relationships emerge as catalysts for overwhelming emotional responses. Understanding these triggers allows us to empathize with the challenges faced by individuals with BPD and fosters an environment of support and validation.

Self-harm and suicidal tendencies, though distressing aspects, demand our understanding and compassion. While self-harm may seem perplexing to some, it is important to recognize that individuals with BPD employ these behaviors as coping mechanisms, albeit paradoxical ones. Self-harm provides temporary respite from the overwhelming emotional pain, offering a fleeting sense of control and grounding. It is crucial to emphasize that self-harm is not a suicidal act but rather an attempt to navigate the complexities of emotional turmoil.

In the subsequent sections, we will embark on a meticulous examination of the core symptoms of BPD, exploring the triggers that incite emotional turbulence, and gaining a profound understanding of self-harm and suicidal tendencies. Through this exploration, we hope to demystify the startling truths surrounding BPD and promote greater awareness, compassion, and support for individuals battling this challenging condition.

THE CORE SYMPTOMS OF BPD

Borderline Personality Disorder encompasses a constellation of symptoms that form the foundation of this intricate condition. By comprehending these core symptoms, we deepen our understanding of the inner struggles experienced by individuals with BPD. Let us delve into the key characteristics that define this disorder:

Emotional Dysregulation: Individuals with BPD grapple with intense and rapid emotional fluctuations. Their emotions can oscillate from extreme highs to profound lows within short periods. This emotional rollercoaster often leaves individuals feeling overwhelmed, as they struggle to maintain emotional equilibrium. The intensity of emotions experienced by individuals with BPD can be likened to an amplifier, magnifying even the slightest emotional stimuli.

Impulsive Behavior: Impulsivity is a pervasive

feature of BPD, manifesting in various aspects of an individual's life. Impulsive behaviors can encompass a range of actions, such as substance abuse, compulsive spending, reckless driving, risky sexual encounters, or binge eating. These impulsive behaviors often serve as an attempt to alleviate emotional distress temporarily. By engaging in such behaviors, individuals with BPD may experience a fleeting sense of relief or escape from the inner turmoil they constantly grapple with.

Unstable Relationships: Building and maintaining stable, healthy relationships poses a significant challenge for individuals with BPD. The fear of abandonment, deeply rooted in their psyche, can cause them to experience intense anxiety and insecurity within relationships. This fear often leads to a pattern of idealizing their loved ones, followed by sudden devaluation when they perceive signs of rejection or abandonment. These drastic shifts in perception and emotional intensity can strain relationships, contributing to a cycle of tumultuous dynamics.

Distorted Self-Image: A distorted self-image is a common struggle for individuals with BPD. They often grapple with a sense of identity confusion, feeling uncertain about their core values, goals, and even their fundamental sense of self. This pervasive instability in self-perception can lead to a tendency to adopt different personas or rapidly change their life direction. Individuals with BPD may have a persistent feeling of being lost, disconnected from a stable and cohesive sense of identity.

COMMON TRIGGERS AND EMOTIONAL ROLLERCOASTER

To gain a comprehensive understanding of BPD, we must explore the common triggers that ignite the intense emotional rollercoaster experienced by individuals with this disorder. Although triggers can vary from person to person, there are recurring themes that tend to evoke profound emotional responses:

Abandonment: Fear of abandonment lies at the heart of BPD and can be triggered by both real and perceived threats of rejection or separation. For individuals with BPD, even minor indications of potential abandonment, such a loved one being preoccupied or expressing dissatisfaction, can elicit overwhelming anxiety and distress. The fear of abandonment can set off a cascade of intense emotions, leading to desperate attempts to avoid or prevent abandonment, often through impulsive actions or emotional outbursts.

Rejection and Criticism: Individuals with BPD are highly sensitive to perceived rejection or criticism. Even well-intentioned feedback or seemingly minor slights can be interpreted as personal attacks. The mere suggestion of criticism can trigger a profound emotional response, leading to feelings of hurt, anger, or a desire for revenge. This hypersensitivity to rejection or criticism often stems from an underlying fear of unworthiness or a deep-seated belief that they are fundamentally flawed.

Intense Relationships: Relationships, particularly intimate ones, can be both a source of joy and distress for individuals with BPD. The intensity of emotions experienced by individuals with BPD can create a unique dynamic within relationships. Their fear of abandonment and deep desire for connection can lead to an overwhelming need for constant reassurance and validation. However, the intensity of their emotions and the fear of rejection can result in frequent conflicts and emotional turmoil within relationships. This volatile emotional landscape can strain even the most resilient partnerships and contribute to a cycle of instability.

UNDERSTANDING SELF-HARM AND SUICIDAL TENDENCIES

The topic of self-harm and suicidal tendencies is undoubtedly sensitive and requires an empathetic approach. While these aspects of BPD may be distressing to comprehend, it is crucial to foster understanding and compassion to effectively support individuals facing these challenges:

Self-Harm: Self-harm, such as cutting, burning, or other self-inflicted injuries, is a behavior commonly associated with BPD. It is essential to recognize that self-harm is not a suicidal act but rather a coping mechanism employed by individuals with BPD. Paradoxically, self-harm provides a temporary release from overwhelming emotional pain, as it allows individuals to regain a sense of control over their inner turmoil. It is crucial to approach self-harm with empathy, understanding that it serves as a maladaptive coping mechanism and a desperate attempt to find relief.

Suicidal Tendencies: Suicidal tendencies are a serious concern in individuals with BPD. The emotional turmoil, intense distress, and feelings of hopelessness that often accompany this disorder can lead some individuals to contemplate or even attempt suicide. It is essential to approach this topic with utmost care, recognizing the urgency of providing support, professional intervention, and a network of resources to individuals who may be experiencing suicidal ideation. Addressing suicidal tendencies requires a collaborative effort involving mental health professionals, loved ones, and support systems to ensure the safety and well-being of those at risk.

TAKEAWAYS

As we conclude this enlightening chapter, let us reflect on the key takeaways that have emerged from our exploration of Borderline Personality Disorder (BPD):

Understanding Complexity: BPD is a complex condition characterized by emotional dysregulation, impulsive behavior, unstable relationships, and a distorted self-image. Recognizing the multifaceted nature of BPD allows us to approach individuals with empathy, acknowledging the challenges they face in navigating their emotions and relationships.

Emotional Rollercoaster: The emotional rollercoaster experienced by individuals with BPD can be intense and overwhelming. Being aware of common triggers such as abandonment, rejection, and criticism can help us provide a more supportive and understanding environment for those with BPD.

Compassion for Self-Harm: Self-harm is a distressing aspect associated with BPD, but it is important to approach it with compassion and empathy. Recognizing self-harm as a maladaptive coping mechanism rather than a suicidal act can lead to more effective support and intervention for individuals struggling with this behavior.

Addressing Suicidal Tendencies: Suicidal tendencies are a serious concern in individuals with BPD. It is crucial to prioritize the safety and well-being of those at risk by providing immediate support, professional intervention, and access to appropriate resources.

Fostering Awareness and Support: By deepening our knowledge and understanding of BPD, we can combat the stigma and misconceptions surrounding this condition. Increasing awareness within our communities and promoting support networks can help individuals with BPD access the resources and treatment they need to lead fulfilling lives.

In our collective efforts to unravel the startling truths of BPD, let us remember that empathy, compassion, and education are powerful tools. By fostering a supportive environment and striving to understand the complexities faced by individuals with BPD, we can contribute to a more inclusive and compassionate society.

2 THE ROADMAP TO HEALING

"Healing is a journey, a road we must traverse with patience and self-compassion. Along this winding path, we discover the strength to mend our wounds, the wisdom to embrace our vulnerabilities, and the courage to forge a brighter future."

JOHN MARK GREEN

n this chapter, we delve into the profound and transformative process of healing, as we explore the roadmap that leads individuals with BPD towards a life of stability, self-discovery, and empowerment. We will navigate through the essential steps of diagnosis, seeking professional help, and developing a comprehensive treatment plan. Additionally, we will embark on an exploration of various therapeutic approaches that have shown promise in assisting individuals with BPD on their path to growth and well-being.

Borderline Personality Disorder is a complex and often misunderstood mental health condition characterized by challenges in emotion regulation, unstable relationships, identity disturbance, and self-destructive behaviors. However, it is crucial to remember that recovery is possible. By gaining a deeper understanding of BPD and implementing evidence-based interventions, individuals can experience substantial improvements in their quality of life.

DIAGNOSIS AND SEEKING PROFESSIONAL HELP

Obtaining an accurate diagnosis is a crucial first step towards healing for individuals with Borderline Personality Disorder (BPD). BPD is a complex and often misunderstood disorder that affects the way people think and feel about themselves and others. Individuals with BPD may experience intense emotional instability, difficulty with relationships, and a distorted sense of self-identity.

Given the overlapping symptoms of BPD with other mental health conditions, accurate diagnosis can be challenging, and it is essential to seek the expertise of mental health professionals specializing in personality disorders. A comprehensive evaluation process is typically employed, which involves interviews, clinical assessments, and a thorough review of the individual's medical history. Mental health professionals use standardized diagnostic criteria, such as those outlined in the DSM-5, to assess the presence of BPD symptoms and their impact on the individual's overall functioning. This process aims to ensure an accurate diagnosis, which is critical in developing an appropriate treatment plan tailored to the individual's unique needs.

Seeking professional help is essential for individuals with BPD. Mental health professionals, such as psychiatrists, psychologists, or licensed therapists, possess specialized knowledge and expertise in accurately diagnosing BPD and guiding individuals towards effective treatment options. These professionals provide a safe and supportive environment for individuals to explore their emotions, address underlying issues, and develop essential coping skills.

Collaborating with a skilled mental health professional is an essential step towards healing and recovery. The journey to healing from BPD can be challenging, but with the right support and guidance, it is possible to learn how to manage symptoms and live a fulfilling life. Treatment options may include psychotherapy, medication, or a combination of both, depending on the individual's unique needs. With the right diagnosis, treatment, and support network, individuals with BPD can find hope and healing.

DEVELOPING A COMPREHENSIVE TREATMENT PLAN

Recovery from BPD necessitates a comprehensive and holistic treatment approach that addresses the multifaceted aspects of the disorder. By developing a comprehensive treatment plan tailored to the individual's specific needs, we create a roadmap towards stability and personal growth.

A collaborative treatment approach involving the individual, mental health professionals, and support systems is integral to the healing process. This collaborative effort fosters a therapeutic alliance built on trust, empathy, and mutual respect. Through open and honest communication, treatment providers gain valuable insights into the individual's experiences, challenges, and goals. This shared understanding forms the basis for an individualized treatment plan that takes into account the unique circumstances and preferences of the person with BPD.

Psychoeducation plays a vital role in the treatment of BPD. It involves providing individuals with BPD and their loved ones with a comprehensive understanding of the disorder. Psychoeducation helps individuals recognize and make sense of their symptoms, reducing self-stigma and promoting self-compassion. It also empowers individuals to actively participate in their treatment by gaining knowledge about evidence-based therapies, coping strategies, and self-care practices.

In addition to psychoeducation, skill-building techniques form an essential component of the comprehensive treatment plan for individuals with BPD. These techniques focus on developing and strengthening specific skills that are particularly beneficial for managing BPD symptoms and improving overall well-being. Emotion regulation skills enable individuals to identify, understand, and modulate intense emotions, fostering emotional stability. Distress tolerance skills equip individuals with effective strategies to cope with and navigate distressing situations without resorting to self-destructive behaviors. Interpersonal effectiveness skills provide individuals with the tools to establish and maintain healthy relationships, effectively communicate their needs, and set boundaries.

Furthermore, medication management may be a part of the comprehensive treatment plan. While medication is not a standalone treatment for BPD, it can be a valuable adjunctive approach in managing specific symptoms or co-occurring conditions. Psychotropic medications, such as mood stabilizers or certain antidepressants, may be prescribed to address mood swings, impulsivity, or comorbid disorders such as depression or anxiety. It is important to note that medication should be carefully monitored and adjusted by a qualified healthcare professional to ensure optimal effectiveness and minimize potential side effects.

THERAPEUTIC APPROACHES FOR BPD

Dialectical Behavior Therapy (DBT)

DBT is a comprehensive and structured therapeutic approach specifically developed for individuals with BPD. It combines elements of cognitive-behavioral therapy (CBT) with mindfulness practices. DBT encompasses both individual therapy sessions and group skills training.

In individual therapy, the therapist and the individual work collaboratively to explore and address specific challenges related to BPD, such as emotional dysregulation, self-harming behaviors, and unstable relationships. The therapist helps the individual develop a range of skills for emotion regulation, distress tolerance, interpersonal effectiveness, and mindfulness. Through these skills, individuals learn to identify and manage their emotions, cope with distressing situations in a healthier manner, improve communication and assertiveness in relationships, and cultivate present-moment awareness.

Group skills training in DBT provides a supportive and educational environment where individuals learn and practice skills together. The group focuses on enhancing skills related to the four modules: mindfulness, emotion regulation, interpersonal effectiveness, and distress tolerance. The group members receive guidance from a trained therapist, engage in role-plays, and participate in exercises aimed at building skills and integrating them into daily life.

Cognitive-Behavioral Therapy (CBT)

CBT is a goal-oriented therapeutic approach that emphasizes the connection between thoughts, emotions, and behaviors. In the context of BPD, CBT aims to identify and challenge negative or maladaptive thought patterns, beliefs, and assumptions that contribute to emotional distress and problematic behaviors.

The therapist works with the individual to examine and reevaluate their cognitive processes, helping them develop more accurate and balanced thinking patterns. Through cognitive restructuring techniques, individuals learn to identify and replace negative thoughts with more adaptive and realistic ones. This process enables individuals to gain control over their emotions, reduce impulsive behaviors, and develop healthier coping strategies.

CBT for BPD also incorporates behavioral interventions to target specific behaviors associated with the disorder. The therapist helps individuals identify triggers and develop alternative responses, reinforcing positive behaviors and discouraging maladaptive ones. By actively engaging in CBT, individuals acquire effective coping strategies, develop problem-solving skills, and improve their emotional regulation.

Schema Therapy

Schema therapy is a longer-term therapeutic approach that focuses on identifying and modifying maladaptive schemas or negative core beliefs that developed in early life and contribute to the difficulties experienced by individuals with BPD.

Schemas are deeply ingrained patterns of thoughts, feelings, and behaviors that shape our self-perception and influence how we interact with others. In schema therapy, the therapist helps individuals identify their maladaptive schemas, understand how they impact their current experiences, and develop strategies to challenge and modify them.

Through cognitive, experiential, and behavioral techniques, individuals work to meet their unmet emotional needs, develop healthier coping mechanisms, and foster more positive relationships. This therapy often involves imagery, role-playing, and other experiential exercises to help individuals process and reframe past experiences that contribute to their negative schemas.

Schema therapy also emphasizes the therapeutic relationship between the therapist and the individual. The therapist provides a nurturing and validating environment, offering support and empathy while challenging maladaptive behaviors and beliefs. Over time, individuals develop healthier coping strategies, a more positive self-concept, and improved interpersonal functioning.

Psychodynamic Therapy

Psychodynamic therapy explores the unconscious patterns and dynamics that underlie an individual's thoughts, emotions, and behaviors. For individuals with BPD, this therapeutic approach aims to help them gain insight into their past experiences, unresolved conflicts, and relationship patterns.

The therapist creates a safe and supportive space for individuals to explore their emotions, memories, and unconscious processes. Through free association, interpretation, and exploration of transference and countertransference dynamics Psychodynamic therapy helps individuals with BPD gain a deeper understanding of the underlying factors that contribute to their emotional struggles and difficulties in relationships. By uncovering and processing unconscious conflicts, individuals can gain insight into how their past experiences shape their present behavior and emotional responses.

The therapist encourages self-reflection, promotes self-awareness, and facilitates the processing of unresolved emotions. Through the therapeutic relationship, individuals can develop healthier ways of relating to themselves and others, address unresolved issues, and work towards resolving internal conflicts.

Psychodynamic therapy often involves exploring early attachment experiences, family dynamics, and significant life events that have influenced the development of BPD symptoms. By bringing these unconscious patterns and conflicts to light, individuals can gain a sense of agency and make positive changes in their lives.

OTHER THERAPEUTIC APPROACHES

In addition to the approaches mentioned above, there are other therapeutic modalities that can be integrated into the treatment of BPD, depending on the individual's needs and preferences.

Mindfulness-based interventions involve cultivating present-moment awareness and non-judg-mental acceptance of thoughts, emotions, and sensations. Mindfulness practices can help individ-uals with BPD develop a greater sense of self-compassion, reduce emotional reactivity, and enhance emotional regulation.

Acceptance and Commitment Therapy (ACT) focuses on enhancing psychological flexibility and values-driven action. ACT helps individuals develop acceptance of difficult emotions and thoughts while taking committed actions aligned with their personal values. This approach can help individuals with BPD navigate the challenges of the disorder and pursue a more meaningful and fulfilling life.

Interpersonal Therapy (IPT) is a time-limited therapy that targets interpersonal difficulties and focuses on improving relationship functioning. IPT helps individuals with BPD develop better commu-nication skills, navigate conflicts, and establish healthier boundaries in their relationships. By addressing relationship issues, individuals can expe-rience greater satisfaction and stability in their interactions with others.

It is important to note that the selection of a specific therapeutic approach or combination of approaches should be based on the individual's unique needs and the expertise of the mental health professional. The therapeutic process is collaborative, and the treatment plan may evolve over time to address the changing needs of the individual.

Overall, therapeutic interventions are a cornerstone of BPD treatment, providing individuals with the tools, support, and guidance they need to develop healthier coping strategies, improve emotional regulation, and cultivate more stable and fulfilling relationships.

Therapeutic interventions for individuals with Borderline Personality Disorder (BPD) are not limited to the approaches mentioned above. Depending on the individual's needs and circumstances, additional therapeutic modalities may be incorporated into the treatment plan. Some of these approaches include:

Group Therapy: Group therapy can be a valuable component of BPD treatment. Participating in a therapeutic group setting with individuals who share similar experiences can provide a sense of validation, support, and community. Group therapy allows individuals to learn from others, practice interpersonal skills, and receive feedback in a safe and structured environment. It can also provide opportunities for individuals to develop healthier relationship dynamics and gain insights into their own patterns of behavior.

Medication: While therapy is the primary treatment approach for BPD, medication may be prescribed to address specific symptoms or co-occurring conditions, such as depression, anxiety, or mood instability. Medications, such as certain anti-depressants, mood stabilizers, or antipsychotics, may help manage symptoms and improve overall well-being. Psychiatric evaluation and ongoing medication management should be conducted by a qualified healthcare professional.

Supportive Psychotherapy: Supportive psychotherapy focuses on providing empathy, emotional support, and guidance to individuals with BPD. The therapist establishes a trusting therapeutic relationship and assists individuals in addressing immediate challenges, managing crises, and fostering self-care. This approach can be particularly helpful during times of heightened distress or when individuals are in the early stages of therapy.

Integrative Approaches: Some therapists may employ integrative approaches that combine elements of different therapeutic modalities to address the unique needs of individuals with BPD. These approaches draw from various evidence-based techniques and tailor the treatment to the specific circumstances and goals of the individual. By integrating different therapeutic perspectives and techniques, therapists can create a more personalized and flexible treatment plan.

Family Therapy: Family therapy can be a valuable addition to the treatment of individuals with BPD, as it involves working with the individual and their family members to improve understanding, communication, and support. Family therapy aims to address dysfunctional patterns within the family system that may contribute to or exacerbate the symptoms of BPD. It provides an opportunity for family members to gain insight into the challenges faced by the individual with BPD and to learn strategies for more effective communication, boundary setting, and conflict resolution.

Trauma-Focused Therapy: Many individuals with BPD have experienced traumatic events in their lives, which can contribute to the development of the disorder. Trauma-focused therapy, such as Eye Movement Desensitization and Reprocessing (EMDR) or Trauma-Focused Cognitive Behavioral Therapy (TF-CBT), can be beneficial in addressing the underlying trauma and its impact on the individual's well-being. These therapies aim to reduce trauma-related symptoms, process traumatic memories, and promote healing and resilience.

Creative Therapies: Creative therapies, such as art therapy, music therapy, or dance/movement therapy, can offer alternative means of expression and exploration for individuals with BPD. These approaches provide opportunities for individuals to engage in creative and symbolic forms of communication, which can help access and process emotions, experiences, and conflicts that may be difficult to express verbally. Creative therapies can promote self-expression, self-discovery, and emotional regulation.

Self-Help and Support Groups: Engaging in self-help and support groups, either in-person or online, can be a valuable adjunct to formal therapy for individuals with BPD. These groups provide a supportive environment where individuals can share their experiences, gain insights from others who have faced similar challenges, and learn coping strategies. Participating in self-help and support groups can reduce feelings of isolation, increase a sense of belonging, and offer ongoing support throughout the recovery process.

Case Management: In some cases, individuals with BPD may benefit from case management services. Case managers can help coordinate and navigate various aspects of treatment and support, such as connecting individuals with appropriate resources, coordinating appointments with mental health professionals, and advocating for their needs within the healthcare system. Case managers can provide valuable support in ensuring continuity of care and addressing practical challenges that may arise during the treatment process.

Peer Support Programs: Peer support programs involve individuals with lived experience of BPD providing support, guidance, and understanding to others who are facing similar challenges. These programs create a safe and non-judgmental space for individuals to share their experiences, exchange coping strategies, and provide mutual support. Peer support can complement formal therapy by offering a unique perspective and a sense of hope and validation.

Psychoeducation: Psychoeducation involves providing individuals with BPD and their support network with information about the disorder, its symptoms, and available treatment options. Psychoeducation aims to increase understanding and awareness, reduce stigma, and empower individuals to actively participate in their treatment journey. It can involve structured educational programs, workshops, or individual sessions with mental health professionals.

Relapse Prevention: Relapse prevention strategies are essential in the long-term management of BPD. Therapists work with individuals to develop relapse prevention plans that outline strategies for recognizing early warning signs, implementing coping skills, seeking support, and preventing a worsening of symptoms. These plans provide individuals with a roadmap to maintain progress, manage setbacks, and sustain their well-being over time.

Holistic Approaches: Holistic approaches focus on addressing the physical, emotional, and spiritual aspects of an individual's well-being. These may include practices such as yoga, meditation, mindfulness, exercise, nutrition, and alternative therapies like acupuncture or massage. Holistic approaches aim to promote overall wellness and can complement other therapeutic interventions by enhancing relaxation, stress reduction, self-awareness, and self-care.

Continuing Care and Aftercare: After completing an initial phase of therapy or treatment, individuals with BPD can benefit from continuing care and aftercare services. These services provide ongoing support, monitoring, and reinforcement of the skills and strategies learned during therapy. Continuing care may involve periodic check-ins with mental health professionals, support groups, or other resources to ensure that progress is maintained and any emerging challenges are addressed promptly.

Crisis Intervention: Individuals with BPD may experience periods of heightened emotional distress or crises. Crisis intervention strategies are designed to provide immediate support and stabilization during these difficult times. Mental health professionals can help individuals develop personalized crisis plans that outline steps to take when faced with overwhelming emotions or distressing situations. Crisis intervention may involve additional therapy sessions, medication adjustments, or accessing emergency services if necessary.

Peer Coaching/Mentoring: Peer coaching or mentoring programs involve individuals with lived experience of BPD who have made progress in their own recovery journey providing guidance and support to others. Peer coaches or mentors can share their insights, coping strategies, and practical tips for managing symptoms and improving well-being. The peer-to-peer connection can foster hope, encouragement, and motivation in individuals seeking to navigate their own recovery.

Community Integration: Integrating individuals with BPD into their communities and helping them build social connections is an important aspect of their treatment. This can involve engaging in social activities, pursuing hobbies or interests, volunteering, or joining support groups or advocacy organizations. Community integration promotes a sense of belonging, reduces isolation, and provides opportunities for individuals to practice and reinforce their newly acquired coping skills and healthy relationship patterns.

Regular Progress Evaluation: Regular evaluation of progress is crucial in the treatment of BPD. Mental health professionals will assess the effectiveness of the chosen therapeutic interventions, monitor symptom changes, and make adjustments to the treatment plan as needed. This ongoing evaluation helps ensure that the treatment remains aligned with the individual's evolving needs and goals, optimizing the chances of successful outcomes.

TAKEAWAY

In conclusion, the roadmap to healing for individuals with Borderline Personality Disorder (BPD) is a multi-faceted and empowering journey. By embracing the crucial steps of accurate diagnosis, seeking professional help, and developing a comprehensive treatment plan, individuals with BPD can embark on a path towards recovery and well-being. It is important to remember that healing is a unique and individual process, and the treatment plan should be tailored to each person's specific needs.

Furthermore, exploring therapeutic approaches such as Dialectical Behavior Therapy (DBT), Cognitive-Behavioral Therapy (CBT), schema therapy, and psychodynamic therapy can provide valuable tools and techniques for managing symptoms, fostering self-awareness, and improving relationships. However, it is essential to work closely with mental health professionals to determine the most suitable approach for each individual.

Above all, the takeaway from this chapter is that healing is possible. With dedication, support, and a commitment to self-discovery, individuals with BPD can navigate their journey towards a more stable and fulfilling life. Remember, seeking professional help, building a strong support network, and engaging in evidence-based treatments are essential steps in this transformative process. Embrace the power within yourself to heal and grow, and know that you are not alone on this road to recovery.

3 DEBUNKING MYTHS ABOUT BPD

"Debunking myths about Borderline Personality Disorder requires challenging stigma and misinformation, promoting accurate understanding and empathy, and recognizing that individuals with BPD can lead fulfilling lives with appropriate support, treatment, and self-care."

MARSHA M. LINEHAN

---

n this chapter, we will explore and dismantle common misconceptions surrounding Borderline Personality Disorder (BPD). By doing so, we hope to provide valuable insights, tips, and personal experiences that will help individuals thrive beyond BPD. So, let's dive in and uncover the truth!

MYTH 1: BPD IS A RARE DISORDER

Contrary to popular belief, BPD is not as rare as one might think. In fact, it is estimated that approximately 1.6% of the adult population in the United States alone is affected by BPD. This means that millions of individuals around the world are living with this condition. BPD is more common than you might realize, and you are not alone in your journey.

MYTH 2: PEOPLE WITH BPD ARE MANIPULATIVE AND ATTENTION-SEEKING

One of the most harmful myths about BPD is the assumption that individuals with this condition are inherently manipulative and attention-seeking. This stereotype not only perpetuates stigma but also fails to acknowledge the deep emotional struggles experienced by people with BPD. The truth is that BPD is characterized by intense emotions and a profound fear of abandonment. It is important to recognize that the behaviors associated with BPD often stem from a desperate need for validation and a fear of rejection.

MYTH 3: PEOPLE WITH BPD CANNOT MAINTAIN HEALTHY RELATIONSHIPS

Another common myth about BPD is that individuals with this condition are incapable of maintaining healthy and fulfilling relationships. While it is true that BPD can present challenges in interpersonal dynamics, it is not an insurmountable obstacle. With the right understanding, support, and tools, individuals with BPD can learn to cultivate healthy relationships. Strategies such as effective communication, boundary-setting, and emotional regulation can greatly contribute to building and nurturing successful connections.

MYTH 4: PD IS UNTREATABLE AND INDIVIDUALS CANNOT RECOVER

Contrary to the belief that BPD is untreatable, there are various treatment options available that can significantly improve the lives of individuals with this condition. Therapy, such as Dialectical Behavior

Therapy (DBT), has shown great success in helping individuals with BPD develop coping mechanisms, regulate emotions, and enhance their overall well-being. Medications can also be prescribed to manage specific symptoms associated with BPD, such as mood swings or anxiety.

Additionally, it is essential to highlight that recovery is possible for individuals with BPD. While the journey may be challenging, many individuals have not only learned to manage their symptoms but have also experienced a significant improvement in their quality of life. Recovery is a unique process for each person, and it often involves a combination of therapy, self-reflection, support from loved ones, and personal growth.

MYTH 5: BPD IS THE RESULT OF A CHARACTER FLAW OR PERSONAL WEAKNESS

It is crucial to debunk the myth that BPD is a result of a character flaw or personal weakness. BPD is a complex condition that is influenced by a combination of genetic, environmental, and biological factors. Individuals with BPD are not morally deficient or intentionally difficult. Understanding the underlying causes of BPD can foster empathy and compassion towards those who are affected by it. It is important to support individuals with BPD and help them access the resources they need to manage their symptoms effectively.

MYTH 6: INDIVIDUALS WITH BPD ARE ALWAYS ANGRY AND AGGRESSIVE

Contrary to this myth, not all individuals with BPD are constantly angry or aggressive. While emotional dysregulation is a characteristic of BPD, it does not mean that individuals with BPD are perpetually irritable or prone to violence. The emotional intensity experienced by individuals with BPD can manifest in various ways, including sadness, fear, emptiness, or even joy. It is important to recognize and understand the full spectrum of emotions that individuals with BPD may experience.

MYTH 7: BPD IS A LIFELONG SENTENCE WITH NO HOPE FOR IMPROVEMENT

This myth perpetuates a sense of hopelessness for individuals with BPD. The reality is that BPD is a highly treatable condition, and many individuals experience significant improvements in their symptoms over time. While recovery looks different for everyone, it is important to recognize that with proper support, therapy, and self-care, individuals with BPD can lead fulfilling and meaningful lives.

MYTH 8: BPD ONLY AFFECTS WOMEN

BPD is often associated with women, but this myth overlooks the fact that men can also be diagnosed with BPD. While it is true that BPD is more commonly diagnosed in women, research suggests that men may be underdiagnosed due to various factors, including differences in symptom presentation and societal biases. It is crucial to recognize that BPD can affect individuals of any gender.

MYTH 9: PEOPLE WITH BPD CANNOT HOLD DOWN A JOB OR PURSUE EDUCATION

This myth unfairly assumes that individuals with BPD are incapable of achieving professional or educational success. While BPD can present challenges in the workplace or academic settings, many individuals with BPD are highly capable and successful in their careers or educational pursuits. With appropriate support, accommodations, and self-care strategies, individuals with BPD can thrive and excel in various domains of life.

MYTH 10: BPD IS THE SAME AS BIPOLAR DISORDER

BPD is often confused with bipolar disorder, leading to misunderstandings and misconceptions. While both conditions involve mood disturbances, they are distinct disorders with different diagnostic criteria and treatment approaches. Bipolar disorder is characterized by alternating periods of elevated mood (mania or hypomania) and depression, whereas BPD is primarily characterized by difficulties in emotional regulation, self-image, and interpersonal relationships. Understanding the differences between the two conditions is crucial for accurate diagnosis and effective treatment.

Takeaways

- Borderline Personality Disorder (BPD) is a more prevalent condition than commonly believed, affecting a significant portion of the population.

- Individuals with BPD should not be stigmatized or labeled as manipulative or attention-seeking. Their behaviors stem from deep emotional struggles and a fear of abandonment.

- Despite the challenges BPD may present, individuals can learn to cultivate healthy relationships through effective communication, boundary-setting, and emotional regulation.

- Treatment options, such as therapy (e.g., Dialectical Behavior Therapy) and medications, can significantly improve the lives of individuals with BPD, and recovery is possible.

- It is crucial to understand that BPD is not caused by personal weakness or character flaws. It is a complex condition influenced by genetic, environmental, and biological factors.

- Additional debunked myths include the misconceptions that individuals with BPD are perpetually angry or aggressive, that there is no hope for improvement, that BPD exclusively affects women, that individuals with BPD cannot pursue education or maintain employment, and that BPD is synonymous with bipolar disorder.

By challenging these myths and providing accurate information, we can foster understanding, empathy, and support for individuals with BPD. It is essential to reduce stigma and create an environment that empowers individuals with BPD to thrive and lead fulfilling lives. With the right support, treatment, and self-care, individuals with BPD can overcome challenges, experience personal growth, and embrace a future filled with hope and resilience.

4 CULTIVATING EMOTIONAL RESILIENCE

"Emotional resilience is not about avoiding diffi-cult emotions; it's about cultivating the strength to navigate through them with grace and courage."

BRENÉ BROWN

Alright, folks, buckle up and get ready for a transformative ride as we dive deep into the world of cultivating emotional resilience for all you badass individuals rocking Borderline Personality Disorder (BPD). We're about to uncover the secrets to managing those intense emotions, taming those impulsive tendencies, and building a solid foundation of healthy coping mechanisms and emotional regulation skills. Are you ready to level up your emotional game and kick BPD's ass? Let's dive right in!

Now, we all know that BPD can be a rollercoaster of emotions, am I right? One moment, you're riding the highest of highs, and the next, you're crashing down like a freight train. It's like being on an emotional tightrope, trying to maintain your balance amidst a swirling storm of feelings. But fear not, my friends, because cultivating emotional resilience is the secret sauce that can help you weather any storm and come out stronger on the other side.

So, let's start with the first challenge: managing those intense emotions and impulsive tendencies. We've all been there, feeling like a pressure cooker about to explode. But guess what? You've got the power within you to tame that wild emotional beast. It's all about self-awareness, my friends. Can you identify your triggers? What sets off that emotional firework show? Take a moment to reflect and jot down those triggers. By knowing what pushes your buttons, you can start to take control.

Now, let's talk about emotional regulation strategies. Mindfulness, baby! Ever tried meditation or deep breathing exercises? It's time to bring out your inner Zen master. Mindfulness helps you stay present in the moment, observing your emotions without judgment. It's like pressing the pause button on that emotional whirlwind and giving yourself a moment to breathe. Trust me, it works wonders.

But we're not stopping there, folks. Oh no, we're just getting started. We're gonna reframe those negative thoughts and beliefs like a boss. It's time to challenge those irrational notions that keep fueling the emotional fire. Ask yourself, "Is there solid evidence supporting these thoughts?" Are there alternative ways to view the situation? By shifting your perspective, you can break free from those emotional chains and gain a fresh outlook.

Now, let's move on to building healthy coping mechanisms. When life throws you curveballs, how do you handle it? Do you have any go-to strategies that bring you comfort and relief? Maybe it's hitting the gym and sweating out those frustrations. Or perhaps it's reaching out to your support crew, those trusted friends or family members who have your back. And hey, have you ever considered joining a therapy group specifically tailored for fellow BPD warriors? Sometimes, sharing your experiences with like-minded folks can be downright therapeutic.

Oh, and don't forget about self-care, my friends. It's time to prioritize numero uno – you! Engage in activities that bring you joy, relaxation, and rejuvenation. Treat yourself to some well-deserved pampering. Take a bubble bath, indulge in your favorite hobby, or simply take a moment to bask in the sunshine and appreciate the beauty around you. You deserve it, my friend.

Last but certainly not least, let's enhance those emotional regulation skills. It's time to amp up your self-awareness game. Can you spot the early signs of emotional turbulence? The twitch in your eye, the clenching of your fists – these little cues can be your early warning system. Take note and take action. Engage in some quick mindfulness exercises or distract yourself with a healthy outlet. Remember, you're in control.

So, my fellow BPD warriors, are you ready to embrace the journey towards cultivating emotional resilience? It won't always be an easy road, but trust me when I say that the rewards are worth it. Picture a life where you have the power to ride the waves of your emotions, rather than being swept away by them. A life where you can respond thoughtfully instead of reacting impulsively. It's within your reach, my friend.

Now, I want you to take a moment and imagine your ideal version of emotional resilience. What does it look like? How does it feel? Envision yourself navigating through life's challenges with grace and resilience. Keep that vision in your mind's eye, because it's going to be your guiding star throughout this journey.

Remember, building emotional resilience is not a sprint, but a marathon. It takes time, practice, and perseverance. There will be days when you stumble and fall, but that's okay. Dust yourself off and keep moving forward. Every setback is an opportunity for growth and learning.

As we dive deeper into this chapter, we'll explore various strategies and techniques that have shown promise in cultivating emotional resilience for individuals with BPD. We'll delve into the power of therapy, whether it's Dialectical Behavior Therapy (DBT), Cognitive-Behavioral Therapy (CBT), or other therapeutic approaches. These therapies can equip you with valuable tools and insights to help you navigate the emotional landscape more effectively.

But let me tell you a secret ingredient to success – it's your mindset. Cultivating emotional resilience requires a shift in how you view yourself and your journey. Embrace the belief that you are capable of change and growth. Embrace the idea that setbacks are not failures, but stepping stones towards progress. Embrace the fact that you are not alone in this battle. Reach out for support, lean on your trusted allies, and surround yourself with a positive and understanding community.

So, my fierce warriors, are you ready to take on the challenge of cultivating emotional resilience? Are you ready to embrace the power within you and rewrite your emotional narrative? I know you have what it takes. With determination, self-compassion, and a willingness to learn and grow, you can cultivate the emotional resilience needed to thrive in the face of adversity.

Get ready to unleash your inner strength, my friends. It's time to rise above the challenges, embrace your journey, and become the resilient badass you were meant to be. Let's embark on this transformative journey together and emerge on the other side stronger, wiser, and more resilient than ever before. The power is in your hands. Let's make it happen.

MANAGING INTENSE EMOTIONS AND IMPULSIVITY

Alright, let's dive deep into the first section: managing those intense emotions and taming that impulsive beast within. We all know how overwhelming it can be when emotions hit us like a freight train, leaving us feeling like we're on the verge of explosion. But fear not, my friend, because there are strategies to help you regain control.

First things first, let's talk about self-awareness. The key to managing intense emotions starts with recognizing the signs and triggers that set you off. Take a moment to reflect on past experiences. What situations, thoughts, or interactions tend to ignite that emotional firestorm? By pinpointing these triggers, you gain the upper hand in preparing yourself and developing proactive strategies.

Next up, we have emotion regulation techniques that are your secret weapons in the battle against emotional chaos. Mindfulness is one mighty tool you don't want to underestimate. It's all about staying present in the moment, acknowledging your emotions without judgment, and observing them like a curious scientist. By stepping back and observing your emotions, you create a space to respond instead of reacting impulsively.

Another technique to add to your arsenal is cognitive reframing. This is the art of challenging those negative thoughts and beliefs that fuel intense emotions. Ask yourself, "Is there another way to interpret this situation?" Challenge the assumptions and explore alternative perspectives. By doing so, you can break free from the cycle of negativity and create a more balanced and rational outlook.

But let's not forget the power of self-expression. Sometimes, the best way to manage intense emotions is to let them out in a healthy and constructive manner. Find your creative outlet, whether it's writing, painting, or dancing like nobody's watching. Expressing your emotions through these channels can provide a release valve and help you gain clarity and perspective.

BUILDING HEALTHY COPING MECHANISMS

Now, let's shift gears and explore the art of building healthy coping mechanisms. Life throws curveballs at all of us, but it's how we handle them that matters.

So, let me ask you, my friend, what are your go-to strategies for navigating the stormy seas of life?

Physical activities can be a game-changer. Channel that energy into something productive. Hit the gym, go for a run, or engage in yoga. The rush of endorphins and the sense of accomplishment can work wonders for your emotional well-being. Plus, it's a great way to blow off steam and maintain a healthy mind-body connection.

Social support is another invaluable resource in your resilience toolkit. Reach out to your trusted circle of friends or family members who understand and support you. Sometimes, simply venting and receiving empathy can alleviate emotional distress. And don't be shy about seeking out support groups or therapy groups tailored for individuals with BPD. There's power in connecting with others who are on a similar journey and can offer insights and encouragement.

But let's not forget about cognitive coping mechanisms. This involves reframing negative thoughts, challenging irrational beliefs, and focusing on the positive aspects of a situation. It's like putting on a new pair of glasses that allow you to see things from a different perspective. So, my friend, ask yourself,

"How can I reinterpret this situation in a way that empowers me?"

Lastly, let's talk about self-care. Oh, sweet self-care, the ultimate act of self-love. Prioritize yourself, my friend. Engage in activities that nurture your soul and replenish your energy. It could be taking a hot bath, savoring a delicious meal, immersing yourself in nature, or pampering yourself with a well-deserved treat. Remember, self-care isn't selfish; it's a vital ingredient in your journey to emotional resilience.

ENHANCING EMOTIONAL REGULATION SKILLS

Now, my friend, let's turn our attention to enhancing your emotional regulation skills. This section is all about fine-tuning your ability to navigate the ever-changing landscape of your emotions with finesse and grace. Are you ready to level up?

First, let's talk about self-awareness on a deeper level. It's not just about recognizing triggers; it's about understanding the patterns and cycles of your emotions. Notice the subtle shifts and nuances. When do certain emotions tend to arise? Are there specific thought patterns or behaviors that often accompany them? By understanding these patterns, you can gain insight into your emotional world and develop strategies to manage them effectively.

One powerful tool for enhancing emotional regulation is developing emotional intelligence. It's like having a built-in compass that helps you navigate the complexities of your emotions. Emotional intelligence involves recognizing, understanding, and managing your own emotions, as well as empathizing with and relating to the emotions of others. By honing your emotional intelligence, you can better regulate your own emotions and navigate interpersonal dynamics with greater ease.

Now, let's explore the concept of emotional flexibility. Life is full of twists and turns, and your emotional landscape is no exception. Emotional flexibility is about being able to adapt and adjust your emotional responses based on the situation at hand. It's about recognizing that emotions are fluid and can change in intensity and direction. By embracing emotional flexibility, you empower yourself to respond to situations in a way that aligns with your values and goals.

Another essential skill in enhancing emotional regulation is developing effective stress management techniques. Stress can be a significant trigger for intense emotions and impulsive behaviors. So, it's crucial to have a toolbox filled with healthy and effective strategies to manage stress. This could include practices such as deep breathing exercises, progressive muscle relaxation, or engaging in activities that bring you joy and relaxation.

Furthermore, let's not overlook the power of self-compassion. It's easy to be hard on ourselves when emotions are running high. But remember, my friend, you're human, and it's okay to experience a wide range of emotions. Treat yourself with kindness and understanding. Offer yourself the same level of compassion you would extend to a close friend facing similar challenges. Self-compassion creates a safe and nurturing space for emotional regulation to take place.

As we wrap up this section, I want to remind you that enhancing your emotional regulation skills is a journey, not a destination. It takes time, practice, and self-reflection. Be patient with yourself as you navigate this process. Celebrate your progress, no matter how small, and keep striving for growth and improvement.

So, my resilient friend, you've embarked on a transformative journey of cultivating emotional resilience. You've learned how to manage intense emotions and impulsive tendencies, build healthy coping mechanisms, and enhance your emotional regulation skills. As you continue on this path, remember that you're not alone. Reach out for support, be kind to yourself, and embrace the power within you.

Now, go forth and conquer, my resilient warrior. Embrace your emotions, face life's challenges head-on, and thrive with unwavering emotional resilience. You've got this.

TAKEAWAY

You've now uncovered the secrets to cultivating emotional resilience in the face of Borderline Personality Disorder. Throughout this chapter, we've explored various strategies and techniques to help you manage intense emotions, build healthy coping mechanisms, and enhance your emotional regulation skills. But remember, this is just the beginning of your journey towards unleashing your inner resilience.

As you continue on this path, I want to leave you with a few key takeaways to keep in mind:

- Embrace self-awareness: Recognize your triggers, patterns, and emotional cycles. By understanding yourself on a deeper level, you can develop personalized strategies to navigate through challenging moments.

- Practice mindfulness: Cultivate the ability to stay present in the moment, observe your emotions without judgment, and respond thoughtfully instead of reacting impulsively. Mindfulness is a powerful tool that can help you regain control and find inner peace.

- Build a support network: Surround yourself with understanding and supportive individuals who can walk alongside you on this journey. Seek out therapy groups, support groups, or trusted friends and family members who can provide a safe space for sharing and growth.

- Prioritize self-care: Make self-care a non-negotiable part of your routine. Engage in activities that bring you joy, relaxation, and rejuvenation. Take care of your physical, mental, and emotional well-being, because you deserve it.

- Embrace flexibility and self-compassion: Remember that emotions are fluid and can change. Be open to adjusting your responses based on the situation at hand. And most importantly, be kind to yourself. Offer yourself the same compassion and understanding you would extend to a dear friend.

Now, my friend, it's time to take what you've learned and put it into action. Embrace the challenges and opportunities that come your way. Trust in your inner strength and resilience. Even on the toughest days, remember that you are capable of weathering any storm and emerging stronger on the other side.

This journey may not always be easy, but you've already taken the first courageous steps towards cultivating emotional resilience. So, stand tall, my resilient warrior, and face each day with determination and grace. You have the power within you to thrive, to create a life filled with purpose, and to overcome any obstacle that comes your way.

Keep learning, keep growing, and keep embracing your journey. You are capable of remarkable things, my friend. Unleash your inner resilience and let it guide you towards a life of strength, empowerment, and emotional well-being.

Remember, you are not defined by your BPD. You are defined by your resilience, your courage, and your unwavering spirit. Now, go forth and conquer. The world is waiting for the extraordinary resilience that resides within you.

5 NAVIGATING RELATIONSHIPS AND INTERPERSONAL CHALLENGES

"Navigating relationships and interpersonal challenges requires the willingness to engage in open and honest communication, the capacity to empathize with others, and the courage to face and address conflict head-on."

JOHN GOTTMAN

Welcome to the wild and wonderful world of relationships. Buckle up, because we're about to embark on a journey filled with twists, turns, and heart-pounding emotions. As someone with Borderline Personality Disorder (BPD), you might have faced unique challenges in building and maintaining healthy connections. But fear not, my friend! Together, we're going to uncover the secrets of navigating relationships like a pro. Get ready for a wild ride that will leave you saying, "I've got this!"

UNRAVELING RELATIONSHIP PATTERNS AND THE FEAR OF ABANDONMENT

Let's start by peeling back the layers and exploring those pesky relationship patterns. Have you ever felt like you're stuck in a never-ending loop, attracting the same type of partners or finding yourself in similar situations time and time again? It's like being caught in a maze, constantly searching for an exit. But here's the kicker—once you understand the patterns, you hold the key to breaking free.

Imagine this: You're in a haunted house, and each room represents a different relationship. As you navigate through the house, you notice a recurring theme—a sense of fear, uncertainty, and a desperate need for validation. It's like walking through a hall of mirrors, each reflection distorting your perception of yourself and others. But fear not, my friend! By recognizing these patterns, you can step out of the haunted house and into the light of self-awareness.

Now, let's talk about the fear of abandonment. It's like a constant shadow, lurking in the corners of your mind and whispering doubts into your ear. Picture this: You're standing on a bridge, and beneath you flows a tumultuous river of emotions. The fear of abandonment is like a strong current, threatening to sweep you away. But guess what? You have the power to build a bridge of self-acceptance and self-love, anchoring yourself against the current and finding stability amidst the storm.

COMMUNICATION STRATEGIES FOR HEALTHY CONNECTIONS

Alright, my friend, it's time to supercharge your communication skills and create connections that withstand the test of time. Think of communication as a dance—a rhythmic exchange of words, emotions, and understanding. Are you ready to take the lead and master the steps?

Let's start with active listening, the secret ingredient to meaningful connections. Imagine you're in a bustling cafe, surrounded by the cacophony of conversations. Amidst the noise, you focus your attention on a single voice—the voice of your partner, your friend, or your loved one. You tune out distractions, lock eyes, and truly hear their words. You immerse yourself in their story, their hopes, their fears. You ask questions, seeking to understand their perspective at a deeper level. And in that moment, the connection deepens, and you become a true partner in their journey.

But active listening isn't just about hearing the words; it's about listening with empathy. It's about stepping into someone else's shoes and experiencing the world through their lens. Picture this: You're standing at a crossroad, and each path represents a different perspective. You choose to take the path less traveled, venturing into unfamiliar territory. As you walk that path, you gain a new understanding of the emotions, experiences, and challenges that shape someone's reality. With this newfound empathy, you bridge the gap and foster a connection that goes beyond surface-level interactions.

Now, let's turn up the volume on assertive communication. Imagine you're on a stage, center spotlight, ready to deliver your lines with confidence and conviction. Your words are a symphony, each note carefully chosen to express your needs, desires, and boundaries. You speak your truth, without fear of judgment or rejection, and invite others to do the same. It's like conducting an orchestra of understanding and respect, where each voice is heard and valued.

But assertive communication goes beyond speaking up; it's about active expression. It's about using the power of words, gestures, and body language to convey your thoughts and emotions authentically. Picture this: You're an artist, standing before a blank canvas, armed with a palette of colors. With each brushstroke and every gentle stroke, you paint a masterpiece that reflects your inner world. Your words become the paintbrush, creating a tapestry of emotions and thoughts, inviting others into your vibrant, authentic self.

Oh, and let's not forget the power of nonverbal communication. It's like a secret language, spoken through gestures, expressions, and body language. Imagine you're sitting across from someone you care about, and without saying a word, you convey your love, your support, and your understanding. It's the sparkle in your eye, the warmth of your smile, and the gentle touch on someone's arm. It's a silent conversation that speaks volumes, building bridges of connection that transcend words alone.

But here's the real kicker, my friend—communication is a two-way street. It's not just about expressing yourself; it's about creating space for others to be heard and seen. It's about cultivating an environment where open dialogue and mutual respect thrive. So, as you fine-tune your communication skills, remember to be a receptive listener, ready to embrace the thoughts and feelings of those around you.

SETTING BOUNDARIES AND BUILDING TRUST

Now, my friend, let's dive into the world of boundaries and trust—the pillars that hold healthy relationships together. Imagine you're constructing a sturdy fortress, fortified with walls of self-respect and self-care. Each brick represents a boundary you set to protect your emotional well-being. But building these walls isn't about shutting people out; it's about creating a safe space where you can flourish and grow.

Think of setting boundaries as creating a garden. Just like a garden needs fences to keep out unwanted pests, you need boundaries to protect your emotional garden. As you tend to your emotional soil, you establish limits on what you will and won't tolerate. You nurture your needs and cultivate an environment that allows you to thrive. Remember, boundaries aren't about building walls that isolate you; they're about creating a garden that flourishes with healthy connections.

Trust, my friend, is the glue that holds relationships together. It's like a delicate thread, woven through the fabric of your interactions. Picture yourself on a high wire, balancing your vulnerability with the belief that others will support you. It's a leap of faith, but by extending trust and being trustworthy yourself, you can create a solid foundation for deep and meaningful connections.

Now, trust is not built overnight; it's a gradual process. Think of it as constructing a bridge over a chasm. Each step forward strengthens the foundation, and each act of consistency and integrity adds another plank to the bridge. As you and your loved ones walk across this bridge together, you create a bond that can withstand life's challenges and storms.

But here's the kicker, my friend—building

trust starts with trusting yourself. It's about honoring your instincts, valuing your worth, and knowing that you deserve relationships built on trust and respect. So take that leap of faith, knowing that you have the power to cultivate trust within yourself and in your connections with others.

TAKEAWAY

As we wrap up this exhilarating chapter on navigating relationships and interpersonal challenges, let's reflect on the key takeaways that will empower you to forge meaningful connections:

- Embrace the power of active listening: Tune out distractions, immerse yourself in the words of others, and seek to understand their perspective. Through active listening, you become a true partner in their journey.
- Be assertive in expressing your needs: Speak your truth with confidence and conviction, inviting others to do the same. Assertive communication fosters understanding and respect, creating a

harmonious exchange of thoughts and emotions.

- Harness the language of nonverbal cues: Your gestures, expressions, and body language can speak volumes. Use them to convey love, support, and understanding, creating a deeper level of connection that goes beyond words alone.

- Remember that communication is a two-way street: Cultivate an environment where open dialogue and mutual respect thrive. Create space for others to be heard and seen, nurturing a reciprocal exchange of thoughts and feelings.

- Practice patience and empathy: Building and maintaining healthy relationships takes time and effort. Be patient with yourself and others, and approach interactions with empathy, seeking to understand the emotions and experiences that shape each person's reality.

So, my friend, armed with these invaluable tools, go forth and navigate the intricate web of relationships with confidence. Embrace the dance of communication, and watch as connections flourish, understanding deepens, and your relationships become sources of joy and growth.

Remember, you are the master of your relationships. Embrace the journey, embrace the challenges, and most importantly, embrace the incredible connections that await you. You've got this!

6 OVERCOMING SELF-DESTRUCTIVE BEHAVIORS

"Overcoming self-destructive behaviors demands the unwavering commitment to self-awareness, the courage to confront deep-rooted patterns, and the resilience to embrace healthier choices that nurture personal growth and well-being."

MELODY BEATTIE

Within the depths of your being lies a radiant phoenix yearning to spread its wings and soar. It possesses the strength to rise from the ashes of self-destructive behaviors and embrace a life filled with purpose and self-empowerment. In this chapter, we will embark on a transformative journey of overcoming self-destructive behaviors and nurturing a profound sense of self-worth. Are you ready to set fire to the chains that bind you and emerge as a force of resilience and growth? Let us embark on this voyage of self-discovery and healing.

ADDRESSING SELF-HARM AND SUICIDAL IDEATION

Within the darkest corners of the human experience, there exists a flicker of hope—a glimmer that reminds us of our innate resilience. Addressing self-harm and suicidal ideation requires us to approach these profound struggles with compassion, under-standing, and unwavering determination.

Imagine your pain as an uncharted wilderness—a labyrinth of emotions and thoughts, a maze that seems impossible to navigate. But , know this: you are not alone in this wilderness. There are compas-sionate guides, whether they be friends, family members, or mental health professionals, who are ready to walk beside you on this treacherous path.

To address self-harm and suicidal ideation, we must first acknowledge the validity of our pain and the impact it has on our lives. It takes courage to recognize that these thoughts and actions stem from deep emotional turmoil and a desperate need for relief. By embracing vulnerability and seeking support, we create a space for healing to begin.

With the support of our guides, we embark on a journey of self-exploration. We traverse the terrain of our minds, uncovering the hidden wounds and unspoken narratives that contribute to our struggles. It is like uncovering buried treasure—each layer revealing a new aspect of our pain, and with it, an opportunity for growth and healing.

As we delve deeper into our emotional landscapes, we begin to understand the triggers that lead to self-harm and suicidal ideation. These triggers can be unique to each individual—a painful memory, a feeling of overwhelming emptiness, or a sense of isolation. By identifying these triggers, we gain insight into the complex web of emotions that drive our actions.

BREAKING PATTERNS OF IMPULSIVE ACTIONS

Impulsivity can be like a raging river, threatening to sweep us away in its relentless current. It compels us to make choices without pausing to consider their consequences, leaving us feeling disconnected from ourselves and our values. But fear not, , for within you lies the power to regain control and steer your ship towards calmer waters.

Picture impulsivity as a wild stallion, untamed and galloping without direction. It's time to tame this powerful force and guide it towards more constructive paths. How can we achieve this? By cultivating self-awareness and practicing mindfulness.

Self-awareness is the lantern that illuminates the shadows of our impulsive tendencies. It allows us to observe our thoughts, emotions, and behaviors without judgment. Through self-reflection, we begin to recognize the patterns that precede impulsive actions—a surge of intense emotion, a craving for immediate gratification, or a sense of being overwhelmed.

Mindfulness is the anchor that keeps us grounded amidst the chaos of impulsivity. It is the art of being fully present in the here and now, of paying attention to our thoughts and feelings without becoming entangled in them. By practicing mindfulness, we create a space for pause—an opportunity to consider the potential consequences of our actions and make intentional choices.

As we navigate the realm of impulsivity, we equip ourselves with practical strategies to intercept impulsive actions and pave the way for more constructive alternatives. These strategies act as a shield, protecting us from the grip of impulsive behavior and allowing us to make choices aligned with our long-term well-being.

One powerful strategy is the implementation of a pause button. When confronted with an impulsive urge, imagine a metaphorical button that you can press, halting the immediate response and creating a moment of reflection. Take a deep breath, ask yourself probing questions: What am I feeling right now? What is driving this impulse? By engaging in this introspective process, you invite a deeper understanding of your underlying motivations and triggers.

In addition to the pause button, grounding techniques can anchor you to the present moment and provide a sense of stability. These techniques involve focusing on your senses, such as noticing the feeling of your breath, the texture of an object in your hand, or the sounds around you. Grounding brings you back to the present, helping to break the cycle of impulsive actions fueled by past regrets or future worries.

Furthermore, it is crucial to seek healthier outlets for emotional release. Engaging in creative pursuits, such as writing, painting, or playing an instrument, allows for self-expression and catharsis. Physical activities like exercise, yoga, or dancing can also provide a healthy channel for releasing pent-up emotions and reducing impulsive tendencies. Additionally, maintaining a support system of trusted individuals who can provide guidance, understanding, and encouragement can be invaluable on your journey towards breaking free from impulsive patterns.

Remember, , breaking patterns of impulsivity requires patience and self-compassion. It is a process of self-discovery and growth, and setbacks may occur along the way. Celebrate each small victory and acknowledge the progress you make. With time and practice, you will develop the resilience and strength needed to navigate life's challenges with intentionality and mindfulness.

DEVELOPING A POSITIVE SELF-IMAGE AND SELF-WORTH

In a world that often undermines our self-worth, fostering a positive self-image becomes a revolutionary act of self-love. It's time to shed the layers of self-doubt and embrace the radiant essence of your being.

Picture your self-image as a mosaic—a beautiful masterpiece composed of countless unique pieces. Each piece represents an aspect of your identity, your strengths, and your potential. Embrace the complexity and richness of this mosaic, for it is what makes you truly remarkable.

To develop a positive self-image, it begins with self-acceptance and self-compassion. Acknowledge that you are a work in progress, and that imperfections are a natural part of the human experience. Embrace your quirks, your idiosyncrasies, and your past mistakes as stepping stones towards growth and self-discovery.

Challenge the negative narratives that have been ingrained within you. These narratives may have originated from external sources or past experiences, but it is within your power to redefine them. Replace self-criticism with self-affirmation. When faced with self-doubt, ask yourself: What evidence do I have that contradicts these negative beliefs? What are my unique strengths and qualities that contribute positively to the world?

Surround yourself with positive influences. Seek out individuals who uplift and inspire you, who see your worth and celebrate your accomplishments. Engage in activities that nourish your soul and reinforce a positive self-image. Practice gratitude for the qualities and achievements that make you who you are.

Additionally, be mindful of the language you use when speaking to yourself. Instead of dwelling on shortcomings, focus on self-encouragement and growth. Replace self-defeating statements with empowering questions: What can I learn from this experience? How can I use my strengths to overcome challenges?

Remember, , developing a positive self-image and self-worth is an ongoing process that requires consistent effort and self-reflection. It involves peeling back the layers of self-doubt and embracing the truth of your inherent worthiness. As you embark on this journey, consider the following additional strategies:

1. Practice self-care: Prioritize activities that nourish your mind, body, and soul. Engage in activities that bring you joy, relaxation, and rejuvenation. Nurture yourself with healthy food, regular exercise, and sufficient sleep. Taking care of yourself sends a powerful message that you value your well-being and deserve to be treated with kindness.

2. Celebrate achievements, big and small: Recognize and celebrate your accomplishments, no matter how small they may seem. Acknowledge your progress, growth, and resilience. Celebrate the milestones along your path, as they are evidence of your strength and determination.

3. Surround yourself with positivity: Surround yourself with individuals who believe in you and support your journey. Seek out relationships that uplift and inspire you. Engage in communities and activities that foster positivity and personal growth. Remember, the energy you surround yourself with has a profound impact on your self-image.

4. Set realistic goals: Establish goals that align with your values and aspirations. Break them down into manageable steps, and celebrate your progress along the way. By setting achievable goals, you build a sense of competence and confidence, reinforcing your positive self-image.

5. Challenge limiting beliefs: Identify and challenge the limiting beliefs that hold you back. Examine the beliefs you have about yourself, your abilities, and your worth. Ask yourself if these beliefs are based on facts or if they are distorted perceptions. Replace negative beliefs with empowering affirmations that reflect your true potential.

6. Seek professional support: If self-destructive behaviors, self-harm, or suicidal ideation persist, seeking professional help is crucial. Mental health professionals can provide guidance, support, and evidence-based interventions tailored to your specific needs. They can help you develop coping mechanisms, address underlying issues, and navigate

the complexities of self-destructive behaviors.

Remember, developing a positive self-image and overcoming self-destructive behaviors is a courageous and transformative journey. It requires self-reflection, perseverance, and a commitment to your own well-being. You are capable of rising above the challenges you face and discovering the immense strength and resilience within you. Embrace your journey, for you are the author of your own transformation.

TAKEAWAY

As we reach the end of this chapter, let us reflect on the profound journey of overcoming self-destructive behaviors and cultivating a positive self-image. Remember that you hold the power within you to break free from harmful patterns and embrace a life of self-worth and empowerment. Here are key takeaways to guide you on this transformative path:

- Embrace vulnerability and seek support: You are not alone in your struggles. Reach out to trusted individuals, whether they be friends, family, or mental health professionals, who can offer guidance, understanding, and support.

- Practice self-awareness and mindfulness: Cultivate a deeper understanding of your triggers, emotions, and impulsive tendencies. Engage in mindfulness techniques to create a space for reflection and intentional decision-making.

- Seek healthier outlets for emotional release: Explore creative outlets and physical activities that allow for self-expression and the release of pent-up emotions. Maintain a support system of trusted individuals who can provide guidance and encouragement.

- Foster self-acceptance and self-compassion: Challenge negative narratives and replace self-criticism with self-affirmation. Surround yourself with positive influences and engage in activities that reinforce a positive self-image.

- Prioritize self-care and celebrate achievements: Make self-care a priority, nurturing your mind, body, and soul. Celebrate your accomplishments, no matter how small, as they are evidence of your growth and resilience.

- Seek professional help when needed: If self-destructive behaviors persist or become overwhelming, do not hesitate to seek professional support. Mental health professionals can provide specialized guidance and interventions tailored to your unique needs.

Remember, , the journey to overcome self-destructive behaviors is not linear. There may be setbacks and challenges along the way, but with determination, self-reflection, and the support of others, you can emerge stronger, empowered, and capable of embracing a life filled with self-worth and purpose. Trust in your inner strength and continue to nurture the radiant phoenix within you. You are worthy of healing, growth, and a future filled with endless possibilities.

7 HEALING FROM TRAUMA AND PAST WOUNDS

"Healing from trauma and past wounds necessitates the gentle exploration of our pain, the courage to confront our darkest memories, and the unwavering belief in our capacity to rebuild and thrive."

JUDITH LEWIS HERMAN

J ust as a mighty oak tree draws strength from the richness of the earth, so too can you draw strength from the depths of your own being to overcome the impact of trauma. Within the realm of Borderline Personality Disorder (BPD), the wounds of the past can shape the present, influencing thoughts, emotions, and behaviors. But fear not, for the human spirit possesses an incredible resilience, capable of transforming pain into growth and reclaiming a life of joy and fulfillment. In this chapter, we embark on an exploration of healing, guiding you through the intricate terrain of recognizing the impact of trauma, employing trauma-informed approaches to facilitate healing, and developing effective strategies for navigating the realm of emotional flashbacks. So, , take a deep breath, for within these pages lies a roadmap to reclaiming your power, rewriting your narrative, and embarking on a journey of profound healing.

RECOGNIZING THE IMPACT OF TRAUMA ON BPD

Imagine, for a moment, standing at the edge of a vast landscape, where the echoes of past traumas reverberate through the soil beneath your feet. Just as a stone cast into a still pond creates ripples that extend far beyond its point of impact, so too do the traumatic experiences of the past send shockwaves through the intricate tapestry of your being. Reflect, , on the imprints left by these experiences. How have they shaped your perception of yourself, others, and the world around you? By recognizing the impact of trauma on BPD, we shed light on the tangled roots that intertwine with the condition, paving the way for understanding, compassion, and transformation. Through self-reflection and exploration, you embark on a journey of unraveling the threads that bind you to the past, freeing yourself to create a future grounded in resilience and growth.

TRAUMA-INFORMED APPROACHES TO HEALING

Now, let us embark on a journey toward healing guided by a compass of trauma-informed approaches. Picture yourself as an intrepid explorer, equipped with the tools and knowledge to navigate the treacherous terrains of your inner landscape. Trauma-informed approaches provide the guiding light, illuminating the path toward healing, and offering solace in the face of adversity. As we traverse this terrain together, we explore therapeutic modalities that embrace the principles of safety, trust, collaboration, and empowerment. From cognitive-behavioral therapy (CBT) to eye movement desensitization and reprocessing (EMDR), each approach holds the potential to untangle the knots of trauma, fostering resilience and restoring a sense of wholeness. So, , fasten your boots, for the path to healing is before us, and with each step, we uncover the tools to transform wounds into wisdom, and darkness into light.

WORKING THROUGH EMOTIONAL FLASHBACKS

Imagine, if you will, being caught in the grip of a sudden, powerful storm that transports you back in time, enveloping you in a torrent of emotions. These emotional flashbacks, much like the gusts of wind that whip through the landscape, can leave you feeling disoriented, overwhelmed, and disconnected from the present moment. But fear not, for within you lies the strength to weather these storms and find your way back to calm waters. Together, we shall embark on a journey to navigate the realm of emotional flashbacks. Through a toolkit of grounding techniques, we anchor ourselves in the present moment, grounding the tempest of emotions that threaten to engulf us. Picture yourself as a skilled sailor, adept at steering through rough waters, skillfully adjusting the sails to find balance and stability amidst the tumultuous waves. Just as a lighthouse serves as a beacon of light in the darkest of nights, so too can you find guiding principles and practices to navigate the labyrinth of emotional flashbacks.

Through the power of self-awareness, you become attuned to the subtle shifts in your internal landscape. You learn to recognize the signs and signals that herald the approach of an emotional flashback, allowing you to intervene before the storm fully engulfs you. Reflect, , on the sensations, thoughts, and emotions that accompany these flashbacks. What triggers them? How do they manifest in your body and mind? By developing this awareness, you gain the ability to intercept the storm at its early stages, preventing it from wreaking havoc upon your emotional wellbeing.

Now, let us dive into the depths of effective strategies for working through emotional flashbacks. Just as a skilled mountaineer equips themselves with sturdy ropes and climbing gear to conquer treacherous peaks, so too can you arm yourself with an arsenal of techniques to navigate the peaks and valleys of your emotions. From grounding exercises that anchor you firmly in the present moment to self-soothing practices that offer comfort and reassurance, these tools become your allies in the face of emotional turmoil. Consider, , the various techniques that resonate with you. Is it deep breathing exercises, mindfulness meditation, or perhaps engaging in creative outlets such as art or writing? As we explore these strategies, remember that there is no one-size-fits-all approach. Embrace the freedom to experiment, to discover what works best for you, and to build your own personalized toolkit for emotional resilience.

Beyond the individual realm, the power of connection and support cannot be underestimated. Just as a group of mountaineers embarks on an expedition together, offering encouragement and assistance along the way, so too can you seek solace and guidance from trusted individuals. Support groups, therapy sessions, or even close friends and family can provide a safe haven where you can share your experiences, gain validation, and receive compassionate understanding. Remember, , you are not alone on this journey. Reach out and build a network of support that lifts you up, encourages your growth, and serves as a reminder of your inherent strength.

TAKEAWAY

As we come to the end of this chapter on healing from trauma and past wounds, I invite you to take a moment to reflect on the insights and possibilities that have emerged. Healing from trauma is a courageous act of self-discovery, self-compassion, and resilience. It is a journey that requires patience, self-reflection, and a commitment to your own wellbeing. By recognizing the impact of trauma on BPD, employing trauma-informed approaches, and learning to navigate emotional flashbacks, you empower yourself to reclaim your life and create a future that is not defined by past wounds.

Remember, healing is not a destination but a continuous process. It is a journey of self-discovery, growth, and transformation. As you embark on this path, be kind to yourself, for healing takes time. Embrace the support of others, cultivate self-compassion, and celebrate each small victory along the way. You have within you the power to heal, to overcome, and to create a life filled with joy, meaning, and purpose. Trust in your resilience, , and know that the path to healing is illuminated by your own inner light.

8 BUILDING A SUPPORTIVE ENVIRONMENT

"Building a supportive environment requires the commitment to cultivate empathy and compassion, the willingness to listen and understand others' needs, and the dedication to foster a sense of belonging and safety for all."

BELL HOOKS

Creating a supportive environment is crucial when it comes to overcoming self-destructive behaviors. It involves surrounding yourself with a network of people and resources that uplift, guide, and inspire you on your journey toward healing and transformation. In this chapter, we will explore the key elements of building a supportive environment and how they contribute to your overall well-being and progress.

THE ROLE OF FAMILY AND FRIENDS IN THE RECOVERY PROCESS

Family and friends play an essential role in your recovery from self-destructive behaviors. They are your support system, your cheerleaders, and your safe haven in times of struggle. Imagine them as the pillars of a sturdy bridge, providing strength and stability as you navigate the challenges that lie ahead.

Think about the people in your life who have shown unwavering support and understanding. How have they impacted your journey? Have they been a source of comfort and encouragement? Reflect on the qualities they possess that make them reliable and trustworthy. Consider how you can nurture and strengthen these connections to further enhance your support network.

While it may be difficult to open up about your struggles, sharing your experiences with loved ones can foster deeper connections and create an atmosphere of empathy and understanding. By communicating your needs and feelings openly, you invite them to be a part of your healing journey. Remember, vulnerability is not a sign of weakness but a courageous act that invites others to meet you with compassion and support.

SEEKING SUPPORT GROUPS AND COMMUNITY RESOURCES

Beyond the support of family and friends, there is immense value in connecting with support groups and community resources. These groups act as beacons of light, guiding you through the darkness and reminding you that you are not alone in your struggles. They are like a tapestry of diverse experiences, woven together to form a network of understanding and solidarity.

Explore the various support groups and resources available in your community. Are there local organizations or online communities dedicated to providing support for individuals overcoming self-destructive behaviors? Seek out those that align with your needs and resonate with your experiences. Engaging with others who have gone through similar challenges can offer valuable insights, coping strategies, and a renewed sense of hope.

Imagine these support groups and community resources as lighthouses along a stormy coastline, illuminating the path forward and offering a beacon of hope. They provide a safe space for sharing, learning, and growing, where you can connect with others who truly understand the intricacies of your journey. Embrace the opportunity to exchange stories, gain perspectives, and draw strength from the collective wisdom of these communities.

CREATING A SAFE AND NURTURING SPACE

Creating a safe and nurturing space is essential for your healing process. Just as a gardener tends to their plants, carefully providing the right conditions for growth, you must cultivate an environment that fosters your well-being and supports your journey toward overcoming self-destructive behaviors.

Start by assessing your physical surroundings. Is your living space organized, clean, and clutter-free? Creating a tidy environment can promote a sense of calm and clarity. Consider incorporating elements that bring you joy and peace, such as soft lighting, soothing colors, or meaningful decorations. These small changes can have a profound impact on your emotional well-being.

Beyond the physical environment, pay attention to the emotional atmosphere you cultivate. Surround yourself with positive influences, whether it's through uplifting music, inspiring artwork, or motivational quotes. These elements can serve as reminders of your inner strength and resilience. Create a routine that includes self-care practices, such as mindfulness, meditation, journaling, or engaging in hobbies that bring you joy.

Think of your safe and nurturing space as a sanctuary, a refuge from the outside world where you can replenish your energy and find solace. It's a space where you can embrace self-reflection, express your emotions freely, and engage in activities that nurture your well-being. Consider incorporating natural elements, such as plants or a calming water feature, to bring a sense of tranquility and serenity to your space. Surround yourself with items that hold positive and comforting memories, reminding you of your journey toward healing.

Moreover, ensure that your safe and nurturing space extends beyond the physical environment. Cultivate healthy boundaries in your relationships and interactions. Reflect on the people, situations, or triggers that may compromise your progress. By setting boundaries and prioritizing your emotional well-being, you create a protective shield around yourself, shielding you from harmful influences.

In addition, practice self-compassion within your safe space. Treat yourself with kindness and understanding, just as you would treat a dear friend or loved one. Remember that healing is not a linear process, and setbacks may occur. When faced with challenges or setbacks, remind yourself of your resilience and the progress you have already made. Embrace self-forgiveness and use these experiences as opportunities for growth and self-discovery.

As you continue to build a supportive environment, remember that it is a continuous journey of growth and adaptation. The support of family and friends, the connections formed through support groups and community resources, and the creation of a safe and nurturing space all contribute to your healing from self-destructive behaviors.

TAKEAWAY

- Recognize the importance of building a supportive environment on your healing journey.

- Foster meaningful connections with family and friends, communicating your needs and experiences openly.
- Seek out support groups and community resources that provide understanding and shared experiences.
- Create a safe and nurturing physical environment that promotes well-being and emotional healing.
- Set healthy boundaries to protect your progress and prioritize your emotional well-being.
- Practice self-compassion and embrace self-forgiveness as you navigate setbacks and challenges.

Remember, that building a supportive environment requires intention, effort, and an unwavering belief in your ability to overcome self-destructive behaviors. Embrace the power of connection, both with others and within yourself, as you continue on your journey of healing and transformation.

9 NAVIGATING THE STORMY WATERS OF BPD AT WORK

"Surviving and thriving in the tumultuous realm of BPD at work demands a blend of resilience, self-advocacy, and a strategic mindset. It's about transforming the chaos into creative fuel, leveraging your unique strengths, and carving a path towards both personal fulfillment and professional success."

IHSAN AYYUB

Hey there, welcome aboard! We're about to embark on a wild journey together—a journey through the choppy seas of Borderline Personality Disorder (BPD) at work. But don't you worry, matey! With a bit of guidance and a sprinkle of pirate spirit, we'll show you how to steer your ship and conquer those stormy waves like a true buccaneer!

Arrr, so you've got BPD, huh? Well, shiver me timbers, you're not alone! Many swashbucklers out there deal with this condition too. And guess what? You can thrive in the workplace despite the rough waters. Aye, you heard me right! BPD might be a formidable foe, but with a little know-how, you'll be sailing on calm seas in no time.

Now, let's hoist the anchor and set sail on this adventure, shall we?

THE POWER OF SELF-AWARENESS: THE COMPASS THAT GUIDES YOU

The first step to mastering BPD at work is to know yourself like the back of your hook hand. Take a moment to examine your triggers, your emotions, and your reactions. Like a seasoned sailor, you must learn to navigate the treacherous waters of your own mind.

When those storm clouds of emotion start brewin', catch 'em before they turn into a full-blown hurricane. Keep an eye on that compass of self-awareness and chart your course accordingly. Remember, you're the captain of your ship, and with self-awareness as your trusty first mate, you'll be able to steer clear of rocky shores.

SHIPSHAPE COMMUNICATION: SMOOTH SAILING WITH CREWMATES

The art of communication is like a fine-tuned ship—when it's running smoothly, there's no stopping you! But if those lines of communication get tangled like a fishing net, things can quickly spiral out of control.

When you're talking to your crewmates, be clear and concise. No need for a barrage of nautical terms—keep it simple, sailor! And don't be afraid to share your struggles with trusted shipmates. They can lend a helping hand and offer support when the seas get rough. Remember, even pirates need a shoulder to lean on sometimes!

ANCHORING YOUR BOUNDARIES: PROTECTING YOUR PRECIOUS BOOTY

Boundaries are like treasure chests—they hold your precious booty safe from marauders and scallywags.

At work, it's important to set clear boundaries to protect your mental health and well-being.

If a task feels overwhelming, don't be afraid to speak up. You don't have to shoulder the weight of the whole ship on your own. A simple "I could use some help, matey!" can work wonders. And if a crewmate oversteps your boundaries, don't be afraid to raise the Jolly Roger and let them know they've crossed the line.

WEATHERING THE STORMS: COPING WITH STRESS ON THE HIGH SEAS

Blimey! The workplace can be a stormy sea, full of deadlines, demanding captains, and unexpected squalls. When the stress starts raining down like cannonballs, it's time to batten down the hatches and weather the storm.

Find healthy coping strategies that work for you. Maybe it's taking a quick breather in your cabin, listening to some sea shanties, or confiding in a trusted friend. And remember, even the most skilled sailors face rough seas. Cut yourself some slack, me matey—you're doing your best!

CHARTING YOUR COURSE TO SUCCESS: GOALS, DIRECTION, AND TREASURE

Every seasoned sailor knows the importance of setting a course and steering toward a destination. And it's no different when it comes to thriving with BPD at work. Set your sights on the treasure you seek—a promotion, a new project, or personal growth—and plot a course to reach it.

Break down your goals into smaller, manageable tasks. Like digging for buried treasure, take one shovel at a time. And don't be discouraged if the X on the map seems far away. Remember, even the longest journey starts with a single step.

ADAPTING TO CHANGING TIDES: FLEXIBILITY IN THE WORKPLACE

The winds of change can blow in unexpected directions, and the workplace is no different. To stay afloat, you must embrace the art of adaptability. Bend like a palm tree in a storm, and you'll weather any gale that comes your way.

Be open to new ideas, strategies, and ways of doing things. Sometimes, the tide might take you on a different path, but that doesn't mean you're off course. Adaptability is the compass that allows you to navigate uncharted waters and discover new treasures along the way.

SEEKING SUPPORT: BUILDING A CREW OF ALLIES

No pirate ever sailed the seas alone, and the same goes for dealing with BPD at work. Surround yourself with a loyal crew of allies who can provide support, guidance, and a shoulder to lean on when the going gets tough.

Share your journey with those you trust, whether it's a sympathetic supervisor, a trusted colleague, or a fellow buccaneer who understands the challenges you face. Together, you can navigate the treacherous waters and conquer any storm that comes your way.

CELEBRATING VICTORIES: RAISING THE JOLLY ROGER

In the midst of the battles you face, don't forget to celebrate your victories, no matter how small. Every conquered challenge is a cause for celebration, so raise the Jolly Roger high and let the world know you're a force to be reckoned with!

Give yourself a pat on the back, treat yourself to a little indulgence, or share your success with your crewmates. Remember, you've come a long way, and you deserve to revel in the glory of your triumphs.

EMBRACING SELF-CARE: NURTURING YOUR INNER CAPTAIN

As a pirate sailing the high seas of work, you must tend to your own well-being like you would the ship. Take time to care for yourself, matey! Engage in activities that bring you joy and help you recharge your batteries.

Whether it's a walk on the beach, a cup of grog, or a good old-fashioned belly laugh, prioritize self-care. Remember, a well-nurtured captain is better equipped to face any challenge that comes their way.

SETTING SAIL FOR A BRIGHT FUTURE: ANCHORS AWEIGH!

We've reached the final leg of our journey. It's time to set sail for a bright future beyond BPD at work. You've learned to navigate the stormy seas, communicate with your crewmates, protect your boundaries, weather the storms, and chart your course to success.

Now, take a deep breath, hoist those sails high, and let the wind carry you toward new horizons. Remember, you're a resilient pirate who can conquer any challenge that comes your way. Anchors aweigh, me hearties! It's time to unleash your inner pirate and set sail for the bright future that awaits you beyond BPD at work.

EMBRACING GROWTH AND LEARNING: BECOMING A SAVVY BUCCANEER

The journey doesn't end here. To thrive beyond BPD at work, embrace a lifelong mindset of growth and learning. Seek out opportunities for professional development, expand your skill set, and keep up with industry trends.

Remember, even the most seasoned buccaneers had to start as landlubbers. It's the desire to learn, adapt, and grow that turns a novice sailor into a savvy buccaneer. So, be open to new knowledge, sharpen your cutlass, and continue honing your skills as you sail towards a bright future.

INSPIRING OTHERS: SHARING YOUR TALE OF TRIUMPH

As you navigate the seas of BPD at work and emerge victorious, remember that your story can inspire others who face similar challenges. Your journey has the power to give hope, offer guidance, and let others know they are not alone.

Share your tale of triumph with empathy and compassion. Whether it's through mentoring, advocating for mental health awareness, or simply lending a sympathetic ear, your experiences can make a difference in the lives of others. Be a lighthouse guiding fellow sailors to safe shores.

SPREADING KINDNESS AND COMPASSION: THE TREASURE OF EMPATHY

In a world where swords clash and cannons roar, never forget the power of kindness and compassion. Be a beacon of light in the workplace, showing empathy towards your crewmates, understanding their struggles, and offering a helping hand.

A simple act of kindness can brighten someone's day, soothe the troubled waters, and create a supportive environment where everyone can thrive. Remember, we're all in this together, sailing through the same sea. Let empathy be the wind that carries us towards harmony and success.

EMBRACING BALANCE: FINDING CALM IN THE SWELLS

Amidst the hustle and bustle of the workplace, it's crucial to find balance, me hearties. Like a seasoned sailor, learn to navigate the swells of work and self-care. Give yourself permission to rest, recharge, and enjoy the simpler pleasures of life.

Seek harmony between your professional responsibilities and personal well-being. Take breaks, indulge in hobbies, and spend quality time with loved ones. Remember, a balanced pirate is a happier, more fulfilled pirate.

YOUR JOURNEY CONTINUES: A NEVER-ENDING ADVENTURE

As we come to the end of this chapter book, remember that your journey doesn't stop here. Each day brings new challenges and opportunities for growth. Keep the spirit of resilience, courage, and determination alive within you.

Set your sights on the horizon, ready to face whatever storms or calms come your way. Trust in your abilities, lean on your support network, and embrace the adventure that lies ahead. With BPD at work, you have the power to rise above the waves and chart a course to a fulfilling and successful career.

Fair winds and following seas, me hearties! May your voyage be filled with triumph, joy, and the spoils of victory as you navigate the world beyond BPD at work.

TAKEAWAYS

- Self-awareness is your compass: Understand your triggers, emotions, and reactions to navigate the workplace effectively.
- Smooth communication sets sail: Keep your communication clear, concise, and open with your crewmates to avoid misunderstandings.
- Protect your boundaries like precious booty: Set and enforce boundaries to

safeguard your mental health and well-being.

- Weather the storms with coping strategies: Find healthy ways to cope with stress at work, allowing you to stay resilient in the face of challenges.
- Set goals and chart your course: Break down your objectives into achievable steps and stay focused on your professional aspirations.
- Adaptability is your lifeboat: Embrace flexibility and adapt to changing circumstances to navigate uncharted waters successfully.
- Build a crew of allies: Seek support from trusted colleagues and supervisors who can provide guidance and understanding.
- Celebrate your victories: Acknowledge and reward yourself for overcoming obstacles, no matter how small.
- Prioritize self-care: Take care of your physical and mental well-being, ensuring you have the strength to tackle work challenges.
- Embrace growth and inspire others: Continually learn, grow, and share your

triumphs to inspire and support others in similar situations.

- Spread kindness and compassion: Show empathy towards others, creating a supportive and harmonious work environment.
- Seek balance between work and personal life: Find a healthy equilibrium that allows you to excel professionally while nurturing your personal well-being.

Remember, this journey is ongoing. The lessons and insights provided in this chapter book are your treasure map to navigate the seas of BPD at work. May you embark on your voyage with resilience, compassion, and the determination to thrive beyond the challenges you may face.

10 THRIVING BEYOND BPD

> *"Thriving beyond Borderline Personality Disorder involves embracing self-acceptance and self-compassion, cultivating resilience and emotional regulation, and forging meaningful connections with others as we navigate our unique journey of healing and growth."*

KIERA VAN GELDER

I n the following pages, we will delve into three key areas that are crucial for not only surviving but thriving beyond BPD. We'll begin by discussing the importance of embracing your identity and authenticity. By celebrating your unique self, you can break free from society's labels and express yourself fearlessly.

Next, we'll explore the significance of cultivating meaningful relationships. Connecting with others who accept and support you can be a powerful source of strength and growth. We'll discuss how to seek your tribe, nourish relationships with authenticity and vulnerability, and establish healthy boundaries.

Finally, we'll delve into the realm of personal growth and wellness. We'll emphasize the significance of self-care as a language of self-love and highlight the transformative power of embracing change and pursuing continuous learning. We'll also celebrate the progress you make, both big and small, on your journey towards thriving beyond BPD.

Throughout this chapter, we'll use engaging language, colorful metaphors, and relatable examples to make the information accessible and enjoyable. So, buckle up and get ready to embark on a journey that will inspire and empower you.

Remember, thriving beyond BPD is not only possible but within your reach. By embracing your identity, cultivating meaningful relationships, and pursuing personal growth and wellness, you can unlock the door to a fulfilling and vibrant life. Let's dive in and discover the wonders that await you on this transformative path.

Now, let's begin by exploring the importance of embracing identity and authenticity.

EMBRACING IDENTITY AND AUTHENTICITY

Embrace the Wildly Unique You!

In a world that often encourages conformity, it takes courage to embrace your true self. But let me tell you, you are a masterpiece of individuality, like a kaleidoscope of colors that can't be replicated. Embrace the wildly unique you, and let your authenticity shine like a shooting star across the night sky.

You're not here to blend in like a grain of sand on a beach. You're here to stand out like a dazzling peacock, captivating the world with your true colors!

Break Free from Society's Labels

Society loves to put labels on people, sticking them on like price tags in a store. But you are not an item to be labeled and shelved. You are a vibrant soul with boundless potential. It's time to break free from society's limited expectations and define yourself on your own terms.

Labels are like tangled headphones. They may try to knot you up and restrict your movement, but remember, you have the power to untangle the mess and find your own rhythm!

Express Yourself Fearlessly

You have a voice that deserves to be heard, like a lion's roar echoing through the savannah. Don't be afraid to express yourself fearlessly. Whether through art, music, writing, or any other form of self-expression, let your inner thoughts and emotions dance freely in the spotlight.

Your expression is like a symphony of emotions, playing the melody of your soul. So, grab that microphone and sing your heart out, metaphorically or literally!

Embrace Your Flaws and Imperfections

Perfection is an illusion, my friend. It's like chasing a rainbow's end—it may look enticing, but it's forever out of reach. Instead, embrace your flaws and imperfections, for they are the brushstrokes that make your portrait unique. Remember, it's the cracks in a ceramic vase that allow the light to shine through.

Embracing your flaws is like adding spice to a

dish—it makes life flavorful and interesting. So, celebrate your quirks and embrace the beautiful mess that is you!

Now that you've learned the importance of embracing identity and authenticity, let's move on to the next chapter: Cultivating Meaningful Relationships. These connections will be your anchor and support system on your journey of thriving beyond BPD.

CULTIVATING MEANINGFUL RELATIONSHIPS

Seek Your Tribe, Your Ride-or-Die Squad

Life is meant to be shared with those who truly understand and appreciate you. Seek out your tribe, your ride-or-die squad—the people who light up your world and accept you for who you are, no matter what. They are the ones who will have your back through thick and thin, cheering you on as you navigate the challenges of life.

Your tribe is like a constellation in the night sky. Each person is a shining star that adds brightness and meaning to your journey. So, gather around the campfire of friendship and let the warmth of connection fuel your soul!

Nourish Relationships with Authenticity and Vulnerability

Meaningful relationships thrive on authenticity and vulnerability. It's about being real, like an open book, and allowing others to see your true self—the beautiful, imperfect, and vulnerable being beneath the surface. When you let down your guard and share your deepest thoughts and emotions, you create a space for genuine connection to blossom.

Vulnerability is like a trust fall. It requires bravery and trust, but when you take that leap, you'll find that there are people ready to catch you and hold you tight. Let your vulnerability be the bridge that brings you closer to others!

Establish Healthy Boundaries

Boundaries are your superpower shield, protecting your emotional well-being and preserving your sense of self. Establishing healthy boundaries is crucial in any relationship. It's about knowing your limits and communicating them clearly, like a skilled negotiator. Boundaries create a safe space where you can thrive and grow together with your loved ones.

Think of boundaries as the guardian angels of your relationships. They ensure that your needs are respected and that you have the space to blossom into the best version of yourself. So, let your boundaries be like a fortress that safeguards your well-being!

PURSUING PERSONAL GROWTH AND WELLNESS

Prioritize Self-Care: Your Love Language to Yourself

In the hustle and bustle of life, it's easy to put your own needs on the back burner. But self-care is not a luxury; it's a necessity. Prioritize self-care as your love language to yourself. Find activities that bring you joy, peace, and rejuvenation. It could be taking a bubble bath, going for a nature walk, practicing mindfulness, or indulging in a hobby you love. Remember, self-care is not selfish—it's a vital act of self-love.

Self-care is like a refreshing oasis in the desert of life. Drink deeply from its well and let its waters quench your soul!

Embrace Change: Dancing with the Unknown

Change is inevitable, and it can be both exhilarating and scary. Embrace change with open arms, like a skilled dancer gracefully moving to the rhythm. Instead of resisting it, view change as an opportunity for growth, discovery, and transformation. Embrace the unknown, for it holds the potential for a brighter and more fulfilling future.

Change is like the wind that carries you to new horizons. Raise your sails and let it guide you to unexplored possibilities!

Cultivate a Growth Mindset: Learning and Growing

A growth mindset is the key to personal growth and development. Embrace curiosity and the desire to continuously learn and grow. Like a student in the school of life, be open to new ideas, perspectives, and experiences. Challenge yourself to step outside your comfort zone and embrace the beauty of life-long learning.

A growth mindset is like a compass that points you towards new adventures. Let it guide you on the path of discovery and self-improvement!

Celebrate Progress, Big and Small

Every step forward, no matter how small, is a cause for celebration. Acknowledge and appreciate your progress and achievements. Whether it's completing a therapy session, facing a fear head-on, or practicing a new coping skill, every accomplishment brings you closer to thriving beyond BPD. Celebrate yourself like a crowd cheering at a championship game, recognizing the strength and resilience within you.

Progress is like a mosaic of small victories, pieced together to create a beautiful masterpiece. Step back and admire the tapestry of growth you've woven!

TAKEAWAYS

We've explored the importance of embracing identity and authenticity, cultivating meaningful relationships, and pursuing personal growth and wellness. As you continue your journey, here are some key takeaways to keep in mind:

- Embrace Your Authentic Self: You are a unique and remarkable individual. Embrace your true self, break free from society's labels, and express yourself fearlessly. Celebrate your flaws and imperfections, for they are what make you beautifully human.
- Cultivate Meaningful Relationships: Surround yourself with those who uplift and support you. Seek your tribe, nourish relationships with authenticity and vulnerability, and establish healthy

boundaries. Meaningful connections will be your anchor and source of strength.

- Prioritize Personal Growth and Wellness: Take care of yourself, both physically and emotionally. Practice self-care as a language of self-love, embrace change and continuous learning, and celebrate your progress, no matter how small. Remember, personal growth is a lifelong journey.

Thriving beyond BPD is not an easy path, but it is a path filled with resilience, empowerment, and personal transformation. Remember that you are not alone on this journey. Reach out to support networks, therapy, and loved ones who can provide guidance and understanding.

Keep in mind that progress may not always be linear, and setbacks can happen. Be patient and kind to yourself. Each day is an opportunity to learn, grow, and embrace the vibrant, resilient person you are becoming.

As you continue your journey of thriving beyond BPD, remember to cherish your identity, nurture meaningful relationships, and prioritize your personal growth and wellness. The next chapter will delve into discovering inner strength and resilience.

You are capable, courageous, and deserving of a life filled with joy, fulfillment, and love. Keep moving forward, and embrace the incredible potential that lies within you. Onward to your next adventure!

11 RIDING THE EMOTIONAL ROLLER COASTER

"Life's emotional roller coaster takes us on a wild ride, with its ups and downs, twists and turns. But it is in the midst of this thrilling turbulence that we learn to ride the waves of our emotions, finding resilience, self-discovery, and the exhilarating freedom of embracing the full spectrum of human experience."

BRENE BROWN

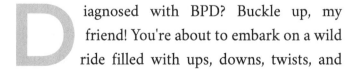 iagnosed with BPD? Buckle up, my friend! You're about to embark on a wild ride filled with ups, downs, twists, and

turns. But fear not! In this chapter, we're going to explore how to process your diagnosis and start thriving beyond BPD.

Picture this: You're on a roller coaster, the wind whipping through your hair, your heart racing. The ride starts with a sudden drop, plunging you into the depths of despair. Your emotions are like that roller coaster, taking you on a wild journey. But remember, just like a roller coaster, it eventually comes to an end.

Processing a BPD diagnosis can be overwhelming. You might feel like a storm is raging inside you, with emotions crashing like waves against the shore. It's okay to feel scared, confused, or even angry. But take a deep breath and remind yourself that this is just a part of your journey, and you're not alone.

One valuable insight to remember is that you are not defined by your diagnosis. BPD is just a label, not the sum total of who you are as a person. You're still that amazing, unique individual with dreams, passions, and a whole lot of potential.

To navigate the whirlwind of emotions, it's crucial to build a support system. Think of your loved ones as your safety harness on this roller coaster. They're there to keep you grounded, offer a listening ear, and provide the encouragement you need to keep moving forward.

Now, let's talk about tips for processing your diagnosis. Imagine you're a surfer riding a gigantic wave. You need balance, right? Similarly, finding balance in your life is crucial for managing BPD. Create a routine that includes self-care, therapy, and healthy coping mechanisms. Think of it as your surfboard, helping you stay afloat when things get tough.

Another valuable tip is to practice self-compassion. Imagine you're talking to your best friend who's going through a rough time. You wouldn't beat them up with harsh words, would you? Treat yourself with the same kindness and understanding. You're doing the best you can, and that's worth celebrating.

Oh, and here's a little secret: you're stronger than you think. It's like discovering hidden superpowers within yourself. BPD might make you feel like you're stuck in a maze, but with time and effort, you'll find your way out. Embrace the journey, because it's shaping you into a resilient and compassionate soul.

In this roller coaster of emotions, remember that it's okay to ask for help. Think of it as raising your hand and saying, 'Hey, I could use a little support here!' Seeking therapy or joining a support group can provide you with tools, strategies, and a network of people who truly get it.

So, my friend, fasten your seatbelt, hold on tight, and get ready for the ride of your life. Processing a BPD diagnosis is challenging, but it's also an opportunity for growth, self-discovery, and building a life you love. Remember, you're not just surviving BPD; you're thriving beyond it!

ILLUMINATING TRUTHS UNVEILED, PAVING THE PATH TO WHOLENESS

n the vast tapestry of the human experience, the intricate threads of Borderline Personality Disorder (BPD) have long remained enigmatic, shrouded in a fog of misconceptions and misinterpretations. But fear not, weary traveler, for within the pages of this enlightening tome, the startling truths about BPD have been unveiled, forging a roadmap to healing that will guide you through the labyrinthine depths of this complex disorder.

As you embarked upon this expedition, you courageously delved into the realms of the mind, where the stormy seas of emotions clash with the jagged rocks of self-identity. Throughout your journey, you encountered the tumultuous waves of intense emotions, the unpredictable tempests of impulsive behaviors, and the haunting echoes of past wounds. However, armed with knowledge and fortified by compassion, you ventured forth, determined to unravel the mysteries that lay in wait.

With every turn of the page, the intricacies of BPD unraveled before your eyes, revealing the core truths that lie at its heart. You discovered that behind the turbulent facade, individuals with BPD are warriors, battling inner demons while yearning for love and acceptance. Their intensity and sensitivity, once misunderstood, emerged as gifts that, when harnessed and nurtured, can illuminate the world with unparalleled brilliance.

Through the wisdom bestowed upon you by expert clinicians and researchers, you gained insight into the multifaceted nature of BPD. You learned that this disorder is not a moral failing, nor a character flaw, but rather a deeply rooted neurobiological condition that affects the very fabric of one's being. You explored the intricate interplay between genetic predispositions, adverse childhood experiences, and the delicate dance of brain chemistry, all of which contribute to the tapestry of BPD.

Moreover, you delved into the therapeutic approaches that can guide those on the path of healing. Dialectical Behavior Therapy (DBT) unveiled its transformative power, equipping individuals with the tools to navigate the stormy waters of emotions, fostering emotional regulation and interpersonal effectiveness. Psychodynamic therapies revealed the hidden narratives that shape one's self-perception, while mindfulness practices illuminated the path to self-compassion and self-acceptance.

As the journey unfolded, you encountered the shattered fragments of relationships torn asunder by the tornadoes of BPD. Yet, with compassion as your compass, you explored the possibilities of understanding and empathy, forging connections that transcend the tumult, and embracing the healing power of genuine human connection.

Within the depths of this book's pages, you discovered that the road to healing is neither linear nor without its twists and turns. It demands patience, resilience, and unwavering self-advocacy. It calls upon you to confront the shadows that linger within, to mend the fragments of self, and to reclaim your narrative from the clutches of a disorder that once held you captive.

So, as you close this chapter of your journey, remember that you are not alone. The truths unveiled within these words have granted you a compass to navigate the labyrinth of BPD, shedding light on the path to reclaiming your life and stepping into a future brimming with hope and possibility.

Embrace the startling truths that have been unveiled, for they are the keys that unlock the gates of understanding and acceptance. Harness the roadmap to healing, paving the way towards a future where the brilliance of your spirit can shine unencumbered. You possess within you an indomitable spirit, a flame that flickers with the resilience of a thousand suns.

May this book serve as a guiding star, illuminating the path that leads you to a life beyond the constraints of BPD. As you step forward into the unknown, remember that healing is not a destination but a transformative journey—a journey that requires unwavering commitment, self-compassion, and a deep well of courage.

ACKNOWLEDGMENTS

As we reach the end of this journey through the pages of Understanding Borderline Personality Disorder, we would like to extend our heartfelt greetings to all who have joined us on this profound exploration.

To our readers, thank you for embarking on this transformative path with us. We are honored to have shared this space with you, to have witnessed your commitment to understanding, and to have witnessed the growth that has unfolded within you. Your presence and dedication have made this journey worthwhile.

To the individuals living with Borderline Personality Disorder, we extend our deepest admiration and respect. Your courage, resilience, and unwavering determination to heal and thrive inspire us beyond words. May you continue to navigate the intricate landscapes of your inner world with grace and self-compassion. Remember that you are never alone, and that your story has the power to ignite change and foster understanding.

To the families, friends, and loved ones who have supported and stood by individuals with BPD, we express our gratitude and admiration. Your unwavering love, patience, and empathy are invaluable on this journey. Your understanding and willingness to learn have made a profound difference in the lives of those you care for.

To the therapists, clinicians, and mental health professionals who tirelessly dedicate their time and expertise to helping individuals with BPD, we extend our deepest appreciation. Your guidance, compassion, and commitment to understanding have brought hope and transformation to countless lives. Your work is a testament to the power of healing and the impact of genuine human connection.

To the researchers and scientists who tirelessly strive to uncover the complexities of BPD, we express our gratitude. Your dedication to expanding knowledge, refining treatment approaches, and challenging preconceptions is instrumental in creating a brighter future for individuals with BPD.

And finally, to the global community that continues to advocate for mental health awareness and understanding, we extend our warmest greetings. Your efforts to reduce stigma, promote empathy, and foster acceptance create an environment where healing can flourish. Together, we can create a world where individuals with BPD and other mental health challenges are embraced with compassion, support, and understanding.

As we bid farewell, we hope that the insights, knowledge, and understanding gained within these pages will serve as a guiding light in your own personal and professional journeys. May you carry the wisdom and empathy cultivated here, and may it ripple outward, touching the lives of others with compassion and hope.

Remember, this is not the end of the story. It is a beginning—a beginning filled with the potential for growth, connection, and profound transformation. Let us continue to walk this path together, supporting one another, and creating a world that values and uplifts every individual on their journey towards healing and self-discovery.

With heartfelt gratitude and warmest wishes,
Michael Grantwood

ABOUT THE AUTHOR

 Michael Grantwood is an acclaimed author and mental health advocate dedicated to shedding light on the complexities of Borderline Personality Disorder (BPD). With a deep understanding of the challenges faced by individuals with BPD and a passion for promoting empathy and understanding, Grantwood has become a voice of compassion and hope within the mental health community.

Drawing from personal experiences and extensive research, Grantwood has crafted a body of work that explores the multifaceted nature of BPD, delving into its intricacies with clarity and sensitivity. His writing seamlessly weaves together the realms of personal narrative, scientific knowledge, and therapeutic insights, providing readers with a comprehensive understanding of the disorder and a roadmap to healing.

Grantwood's unique ability to blend his personal

journey with professional expertise creates a powerful connection with readers, allowing them to feel seen and understood. Through his compassionate and engaging writing style, he fosters a sense of community and encourages dialogue surrounding BPD, dismantling the stigma that often surrounds the disorder.

Beyond his literary contributions, Grantwood is a passionate advocate for mental health awareness. Through speaking engagements, workshops, and collaborations with mental health organizations, he strives to bring BPD to the forefront of public consciousness, challenging societal misconceptions and fostering a more inclusive and compassionate understanding of mental health.

With a background in psychology and extensive clinical experience, Grantwood offers a nuanced and informed perspective on BPD. His dedication to research and staying abreast of the latest developments in the field ensures that his work remains current and evidence-based, empowering readers with accurate information and practical tools for self-discovery and growth.

Michael Grantwood's heartfelt commitment to understanding BPD, empowering individuals, and fostering a more compassionate society has earned him a loyal following of readers and mental health advocates alike. Through his work, he continues to inspire and uplift, offering hope and guidance to those navigating the complex terrain of Borderline Personality Disorder.

Made in United States
Troutdale, OR
11/07/2023

14383482R00086